A knife thrower in a traveling act slits his wife's throat: murder or miscalculation? A brilliant university student incriminates himself by executing a murder too well. A Chinese businessman avenges the murder of his parents by a Japanese soldier during the war. A group of Buddhist monks protect their embezzlement ring by manipulating an underling's belief in the importance of honor and provoking his suicide.

The Japanese have long had a love affair with the Western genre of the detective story. For the past eighty years they have generated a tremendous output of crime and detective fiction, but very little has been translated into English.

These fourteen stories, arranged chronologically, reflect a changing Japan from the early part of this century to the present. Although certain elements will be familiar to any mystery buff—murderers with no intention of being caught, hapless victims, wiley detectives—there are also decidedly Nipponese traits. For example, the murders are rarely committed by firearms, since there has been gun control in Japan for more than 300 years. Also, the national importance of honor and the tendency to commit suicide, *seppuka*, when honor is lost, is often exploited by a clever killer.

Among the notable authors in this collection are Edogawa Rampo, Taro Hirai's pseudonym, a loose transliteration of Edgar Allan Poe; Ryunosuke Akutagawa, whose story "In a Grove" inspired Kurosawa's classic film *Rashomon*; and Shizuko Natsuki, a highly successful contemporary author who often writes about the clash between outmoded traditions and modern realities in Japan.

John L. Apostolou's interest in the Japanese culture dates back to the Korean War when, as a young, impressionable G.I., he served in Japan and Korea. He has written several articles on Japanese mystery writers for magazines such as *The Armchair Detective* and *The Poisoned Pen*.

Martin H. Greenberg, a professor of Political Science at the University of Wisconsin at Green Bay, has edited more than eighty anthologies of crime and mystery stories.

# MURDER in JAPAN

# MURDER in JAPAN

## JAPANESE STORIES
## OF CRIME AND DETECTION

Edited by
John L. Apostolou and Martin H Greenberg

90-1681

Dembner Books · New York

DEMBNER BOOKS
Published by Red Dembner Enterprises Corp.,
80 Eighth Avenue, New York, N.Y. 10011

Distributed by W. W. Norton & Company, Inc.,
500 Fifth Avenue, New York, N.Y. 10110

**Library of Congress Cataloging in Publications Data**

Murder in Japan.
   1. Detective and mystery stories, Japanese—Transla-
tions into English.  2. Detective and mystery stories,
English—Translations from Japanese.  I. Apostolou, John L.
II. Greenberg, Martin Harry.
PL782.E8M78   1987      895.6′30872′08        86-29121
ISBN 0-934878-87-0

DESIGN BY ANTLER & BALDWIN, INC.

*Acknowledgments, permissions and additional
copyright material to be found on page vi*

# Contents

# Foreword

Even quite well-informed lovers of crime fiction tend to think of the genre as something of an Anglo-American preserve. Pressed to cast the net wider, most would after brief reflection name Georges Simenon as a giant in the field, but as John Apostolou points out in his scholarly and stimulating introduction to this anthology, hardly anyone in the West is familiar with even a fraction of the colossal output of Japanese mystery writers over the past half-century and more. All the subgenres familiar to us have their practitioners in Japan. Classic whodunits are called *pazuraa*, from the English "puzzler," while tough, action-packed stories are, reasonably enough, *haada-boirudo* (hard-boiled). There are police procedurals, private eye stories, and accounts of the exploits of amateur sleuths at least as colorful and eccentric as those of our own tradition. For the Japanese love what they colloquially call *misteri* fiction. The domestic demand is insatiable and the Japanese-language market sustains hundreds of professional authors, many of them in circumstances that must be the envy of all but a handful of their most successful Western counterparts.

An established crime writer can expect a new book to be serialized in a monthly or weekly magazine and perhaps even a daily newspaper read by millions. A first hardcover edition will amount to at least 10,000 copies, and a paperback run to a quarter of a million; while in the case of those in the premier league, those figures will probably be doubled. In spite of the mind-boggling complexity of their written language, the Japanese have achieved the highest literacy rate on earth. Moreover they are book *buyers* rather than borrowers, and the quality and variety of the stories selected for this anthology shows that they are blessed with authors of talent, versatility, and imagination.

In this context the language barrier is a one-way obstacle. Tens of thousands of Japanese can read English with ease for each Westerner able to decipher written Japanese, and for those who cannot, a large and representative selection of our books appear in Japanese translation soon after their original publication. By contrast hardly any work by Japanese authors becomes available in English, which makes this splendid anthology all the more welcome. A well-written and sensitively translated story can convey the flavor of another culture and the ways of life and thought of those nurtured within it with a vivid immediacy never to be achieved by even the most carefully researched work of social anthropology—and provide unmatched pleasure into the bargain. I salute with respect and gratitude the crime writers of Japan and those who have translated, selected, edited, and introduced with such skill the stories contained in this book.

JAMES MELVILLE

# Introduction

The Japanese, arguably the most voracious readers in the world, consume vast quantities of popular fiction. Although romance and science fiction novels are popular, much of what is read in Japan falls in the crime or mystery genre. Japanese crime writers have produced thousands of novels and short stories, but very few—about the equivalent of one month's output—are available in English. In contrast, there is a large steady flow to Japan of British and American mysteries. As a result, detective characters like Sherlock Holmes and Ellery Queen are as well known in Japan as in English-speaking countries.

Japanese crime writers deserve greater exposure to readers in the

West. Conceivably this anthology will help to stimulate interest in their work. Collected here are fourteen stories by ten authors, stories selected to provide an entertaining, and yet meaningful, survey of Japanese crime fiction in the twentieth century.

Discussions of Japanese mysteries usually begin with mention of a short story by Edogawa Rampo, "The Two-Sen Copper Coin." Published in 1923, it is generally accepted as the first detective story written in the Japanese language. However, many Japanese crime stories, including four stories in this book, were written before 1923. In fact, Japanese crime fiction can be traced back to the seventeenth century, an important example being Saikaku Ihara's *Records of Trials Held Beneath a Cherry Tree*. This collection of forty-four very short stories was published in 1689, and is available in English under the title *Tales of Japanese Justice* (1980).

Ihara's book and several similar collections were inspired by historical accounts of Chinese court cases. The hero is always a district magistrate who acts as detective, prosecuting attorney, judge and jury, with emphasis given to the magistrate's wisdom rather than to his skill as a detective. Although these stories were sometimes based on actual cases, fantasy elements are often present. The Judge Dee novels by the noted orientalist Robert van Gulik are modern-day examples of this tradition.

Crime stories in the Chinese pattern continued to be popular until the late 1800s when a great number of translations of Western literature were printed by Japanese publishers. Besides the works of Dickens, Tolstoy, and Dostoevski, mysteries by Edgar Allan Poe, Wilkie Collins, Emile Gaboriau, and Arthur Conan Doyle were translated and widely read. It was an exciting period in Japanese literary history. The impact on writers and critics was profound. Japanese fiction became more serious, more realistic, and more concerned with psychology.

After the turn of the century, a few younger writers, notably Naoya Shiga and Junichiro Tanizaki, began producing crime fiction. But Shiga and Tanizaki, who were to become major literary figures, were not interested in deduction or the classic whodunit. Their crime stories are penetrating studies of the criminal mind, and this interest in motivation, in why people commit crimes, is a recurrent theme in Japanese crime fiction.

By the mid-1920s, Shiga and Tanizaki had moved on to different subject matter and another author, the first we can truly call a mystery writer, arrived on the scene. He was Taro Hirai who wrote under the name Edogawa Rampo. The pseudonym he adopted is a loose transliteration—roughly, *Edgar Allan Poe*—written in Japanese characters. Obviously he was a great admirer of Poe, and like Poe, he wrote detective stories and horror tales. A dominant figure in the mystery field for decades, Rampo also produced considerable critical work and did much to promote the genre. He defined detective fiction as "literature which derives its chief interest from the process whereby some baffling secret, usually related to crime, is solved logically and by gradual steps." Under his influence Japanese mystery writers produced fiction that emphasized puzzle elements and unusual twists.

During World War II, which is usually referred to as the Pacific War by the Japanese, the writing of mysteries was banned by the government. In a time that called for national unity, it was considered unpatriotic to print stories that implied conflict between one Japanese and another. When the war ended in defeat, the people of Japan experienced years of turmoil and despair, a period of food shortages and black market activities. The crime stories of mainstream fiction writers Tatsuzo Ishikawa and Haruto Ko give us some understanding of life during the immediate postwar era.

As conditions improved in the 1950s, a new generation of mystery writers came into prominence. Their leader was Seicho Matsumoto, who advocated a more serious approach to the mystery genre. He championed what was to become known as the "social detective" story and attacked earlier mysteries as nothing but unrealistic puzzles. He urged Japanese crime writers to use a more literate style and to turn away from Poe and Doyle and toward Dostoevski. Many authors responded to his message and accepted, at least in theory, *Crime and Punishment* as their model. In their fiction, they began to delve into such matters as government corruption, industrial espionage, and the operations of the *yakuza*, Japan's organized crime alliance. While other types of mysteries continued to be written, Matsumoto and his colleagues became the dominant faction among the writers of Japanese crime fiction. The last two stories in this anthology, those by Shizuko Natsuki, are good examples of "social detective" story writing, although the ingredients of detection and suspense that mystery fans expect are still present.

In good times and bad, from the depths of defeat to the prosperity of today, the Japanese people have always thought of themselves as members of a national family; and when a member of that family commits a serious crime, it is a matter of real concern. Matsumoto said, "To know motives is very important in this day and age, and to show psychological reasons for crime makes a book literature rather than just a detective story." Interestingly, British author and critic Julian Symons expressed much the same idea when he wrote that the business of the crime writer is "to investigate, with all the freedom the medium permits him, the springs of violence."

The modern Japanese novelists whose works are known in the West usually write very personal, often bizarre, novels that give us abundant details on their individual tastes and idiosyncrasies, but tell us little about life in present-day Japan. Japanese crime fiction is actually a better source of information on the daily lives of the citizens of Japan than are the works of Yasunari Kawabata, Yukio Mishima, and other famous novelists. In a virtually effortless way, the reader of this anthology will learn something about Japanese culture and customs.

Besides the obvious differences that result from a foreign setting, Japanese crime stories are unlike Western mysteries in other ways. For instance, characters in Japanese mysteries rarely use firearms since Japan has had gun control, in one form or another, for over three hundred years. Gun control laws are strictly enforced, and most murders, in both fiction and reality, are committed by means such as knifing, striking with a blunt instrument, poisoning, or strangulation.

With the prominence of ritual suicide or *seppuka* in Japanese history and literature, it is not surprising that suicide is often mentioned in Japanese crime fiction. The plot sometimes hinges on whether a suicide took place or a murder was staged to look like a suicide. Oddly enough, suicide is not as common in Japan as one might expect. Recent figures indicate the suicide rate in Japan, although somewhat higher than the rate in the United States, is lower than that in several European countries.

The traditional importance of honor and the family is reflected in Japanese mysteries. Murder and other crimes are often committed by characters attempting to protect their reputations, to protect the reputations of close relatives, or to save their families from disgrace. As in Western mysteries, the murderer's motive often involves greed, jealousy, or revenge.

Acknowledging his major contribution to the growth of the mystery genre in Japan, the first two short stories in this anthology are by Edogawa Rampo. All the other stories are arranged in the order of the authors' birth dates, meaning they are roughly chronological. This sequence should give the reader a sense of the development of modern Japanese crime fiction from a 1910 story, "The Razor" by Shiga, to two fairly recent stories by Natsuki.

A broad definition of crime fiction was used in the selection process, allowing for the inclusion of stories by non-genre writers. Contained in this book are stories by most of the Japanese authors mentioned above. Three other writers—Ryunosuke Akutagawa, Shotaro Yasuoka, and Kobo Abe—are also represented. For each author, a short preface is included, giving some information on his career and indicating the translations of his fiction that are available in English.

It should be noted that, reversing the order used in Japan, Japanese names in this book are printed with the family name last. This practice is widely accepted, although not standard, in English language publications. The only exception is the name of Edogawa Rampo, which appears in the Japanese order, thus preserving its close similarity to the name Edgar Allan Poe.

Several critical and reference works were helpful in the preparation of this anthology. Particularly useful were Kawataro Nakajima's "Detective Fiction in Japan" in *Japan Quarterly* 9:1

(1962) and *Introduction to Contemporary Japanese Literature, 1956–1970* (University of Tokyo Press, 1972).

I would like to thank some people who made valuable contributions to this anthology. Mark Schreiber and Jiro Kimura provided much information for use in the introduction and prefaces. Violet Margosian and Terry Hagar gave me generous amounts of assistance and encouragement. And finally, special thanks to the librarians of the Los Angeles Central Library for simply doing their jobs so well.

JOHN L. APOSTOLOU
*Los Angeles*
*November 1986*

*Edogawa Rampo* (1894–1965) *is known as the father of the Japanese mystery story. He was greatly influenced by Edgar Allan Poe, as were Tanizaki and other writers of the period, and even took a variation on Poe's name as his pseudonym. The author of the first detective story in Japanese, "The Two-Sen Copper Coin," and leader of Japanese mystery writers for decades, he actually wrote mysteries for only a few years. First he turned to tales of horror and fantasy, and then to novel-length thrillers. Detection was replaced by eroticism and the grotesque, elements that became characteristic of his style. However, he continued to do critical work, often discussing mysteries by Western authors and always promoting the mystery form.*

*Nine of Rampo's short stories, eight of which could be called crime stories, are translated in* Japanese Tales of Mystery and Imagination *(1956). Despite its historical importance, "The Two-Sen Copper Coin" is not available in English.*

# The Psychological Test

## by EDOGAWA RAMPO

### TRANSLATED BY JAMES B. HARRIS

Fukiya might have gone a long way in the world if he had only put his considerable intelligence to better use. Young, bright, and diligent, and the constant pride of his professors at Waseda University in Tokyo—anyone could have seen that he was a man earmarked for a promising future. But, alas, in collaboration with the fates, Fukiya chose to fool all observers. Instead of pursuing a normal scholastic career, he shattered it abruptly by committing . . . *murder!*

Today, many years following his shocking crime, conjecture is still rife as to what strange, unearthly motive actually prompted this gifted young man to carry out his violent plot. Some still persist in

3

their belief that greed for money—the most common of motives—
was behind it all. To some extent, this explanation is plausible, for it
is true that young Fukiya, who was working his way through school,
was keenly feeling the leanness of his purse. Also, being the
intellectual that he was, his pride may have been so deeply
wounded at having to consume so much of his precious time
working that he might have felt that crime was the only way out.
But arc these altogether obvious reasons sufficient to explain away
the almost unparalleled viciousness of the crime he committed?
Others have advanced the far more likely theory that Fukiya was a
born criminal and had committed the crime merely for its own
sake. At any rate, whatever his hidden motives, it is an undeniable
fact that Fukiya, like many other intellectual criminals before him,
had set out to commit the perfect crime.

From the day Fukiya began his first classes at Waseda he was
restless and uneasy. Some noxious force seemed to be eating away at
his mind, coaxing him, goading him on to execute a "plot" which
was still only a vague outline in his mind—like a shadow in a mist.
Day in and day out, while attending lectures, chatting with his
friends on the campus, or working at odd jobs to cover his expenses,
he kept puzzling over what was making him so nervous. And then,
one day, he became specially chummy with a classmate named
Saito, and his "plot" began to take definite shape.

Saito was a quiet student of about the same age as Fukiya, and
likewise hard up for money. For nearly a year now he had rented a
room in the home of a widow who had been left in quite
comfortable circumstances upon the death of her husband, a
government official. Nearly sixty years old, the woman was
extremely avaricious and stingy. Despite the fact that the income
from rent on several houses ensured her a comfortable living, she
still greedily added to her wealth by lending money in small sums to
reliable acquaintances. But, then, she was childless, and as a result
had gradually come to regard money, ever since the early stages of
her widowhood, as a substitute consolation. In the case of Saito,
however, she had taken him as a lodger more for protection than for
gain: like all people who hoard money, she kept a large sum cached
away in her house.

Fukiya had no sooner learned all this from his friend Saito than he was tempted by the widow's money. "What earthly good will it ever do her anyway?" he asked himself repeatedly, following two or three visits to the house. "Anyone can see that the withered old hag is not long for this world. But look at me! I'm young, full of life and ambition, with a bright future to look forward to."

His thoughts constantly revolved about this subject, leading to but one conclusion: *He just had to have that money!* But how to get it? The answer to this question grew into the web of a horrible plan. First, however, Fukiya decided that all successful plots depended on one important factor—skilful and thorough preparation. So, in a subtle and casual manner, he set about the task of getting as much information as possible from his schoolmate Saito about the old woman and her hidden money.

One day Saito casually made a remark which nearly bowled Fukiya over, for it was the very information he had long been yearning to know.

"You know, Fukiya," Saito remarked laughingly, utterly unsuspecting the foul plot that was being nursed in his friend's mind, "the old woman surely is crazy about her money. Nearly every month she thinks up a new place to hide it. Today, quite by accident, I came across her latest 'safety deposit vault,' and I must say she's exceedingly original. Can you guess where it is?"

Suppressing his excitement with an actor's finesse, Fukiya yawned and blandly remarked: "I'm afraid I couldn't even make a guess."

Saito was easily caught in the artful trap. "Well, then, I'll tell you," he quickly said, somewhat disappointed by the other's lack of interest. "As you probably know, when a person tries to hide money he usually puts it under the floor or in some secret cavity or hole in the wall. But my dear landlady's far more ingenious. Do you remember that dwarf pine-tree that sits in the alcove of the guest room? Well, that's the newest place she's chosen to hide her money—right inside the earth in the pot. Don't you think she's awfully clever? No thief would ever think of looking in a place like that."

As the days passed, Saito appeared to have forgotten the conversation, but not Fukiya. Having devoured Saito's every word, he was now determined to take possession of the old woman's money. But there were still certain details which had to be figured out before he could make his first move. One of these was the all-important problem of how to divert even the faintest suspicion from himself. Other questions, such as remorse and the attendant pangs of conscience, troubled him not in the least. All this talk of Raskolnikov, in Dostoevsky's *Crime and Punishment*, crucified by the unseen terrors of a haunted heart was, to Fukiya, sheer nonsense. After all, he reasoned, everything depended on one's point of view. Was Napoleon to be condemned as a mass murderer because he had been responsible for the deaths of so many people? Certainly not. In fact, he rather admired the ex-corporal who had risen to be an emperor, no matter what the means.

Now definitely committed to the deed, Fukiya calmly awaited his chance. As he called frequently to see Saito, he already knew the general lay-out of the house, and a few more visits provided him with all the details he needed. For example, he soon learned that the old woman rarely went out of doors. This was a disappointment. Day after day she remained seated in her private parlor in one wing of the house in absolute silence. If, however, sheer necessity did coax her to leave the comfort of her shell, she would first post her maidservant, a simple country girl, as a "sentry" to keep watch over the house. Fukiya soon came to realize that in the face of these circumstances his contemplated adventure in crime would be no easy matter. On the contrary, if he was ever to succeed, he would have to use his greatest cunning.

For a full month Fukiya considered various schemes, but one by one he discarded them all as faulty. Finally, after wracking his brain to the point of exhaustion, Fukiya came to the conclusion that there was but one solution: *He must murder the old woman!* He also reasoned that the old woman's hidden fortune would certainly be large enough to justify killing her and reminded himself that the most notorious burglars in history had always eliminated their victims on the sound theory that "the dead tell no tales."

Carefully, Fukiya began to map out the safest course of action. This took time, but through the innocent Saito he knew that the hiding place had not been changed, and he felt he could afford to make each tiny detail perfect, even down to the most trivial matter.

One day, quite unexpectedly, Fukiya realized that his long-awaited moment had arrived. First, he heard that Saito would be absent from the house all day on school business. The maidservant, too, would be away on an errand, not to return until evening. Quite by coincidence, just two days previously Fukiya had gone to the trouble of verifying that the money was still concealed in the pot of the dwarf pine. He had ascertained this quite easily. While visiting Saito he had casually gone into the old landlady's room "to pay his respects" and during the course of his conversation had ingeniously let drop a remark here and there referring to her hidden cache of money. An artful student of psychology, he had watched the old woman's eyes whenever he mentioned the words *hiding place*. As he had anticipated, her eyes turned unintentionally toward the potted tree in the alcove every time.

On the day of the murder Fukiya dressed in his usual school uniform and cap, plus his black student's cloak. He also wore gloves to be sure he would leave no fingerprints. Long ago he had decided against a disguise, for he had realized that masquerade outfits would be easy to trace. He was of the firm conviction that the simpler and more open his crime was, the harder it would be to detect. In his pockets he carried a longish but ordinary jackknife and a large purse. He had purchased these commonplace objects at a small general-merchandise store at a time when it was full of customers, and he had paid the price asked without haggling. So he was confident no one would remember him as the purchaser.

Immersed in his thoughts, Fukiya slowly walked toward the scene of his contemplated crime. As he gradually drew near the neighborhood he reminded himself for about the tenth time that it was essential for him *not* to be observed entering the house. But supposing he accidentally ran into an acquaintance before he could reach his victim's gate? Well, this would not be serious, so long as the acquaintance could be persuaded to believe that he was only out taking a stroll, as was his custom.

Fifteen minutes later he arrived in front of the old woman's house. Although he had fortunately not met a soul who knew him, he found his breath coming in short gasps. This, to him, was a nasty sensation. Somehow he was beginning to feel more and more like an ordinary thief and prowler than the suave and nonchalant prince of crime he had always pictured himself to be.

Fighting to control his nerves, Fukiya furtively looked about in all directions. Finally, satisfied that he was still unobserved, he turned his attention to the house itself. This was sandwiched in between two other houses, but conveniently isolated from them by two rows of trees on both sides, thick with foliage and forming natural fences. Facing the house on the opposite side there stood a long concrete wall which encircled a wealthy estate occupying a complete block.

Slowly and noiselessly, he opened the gate, holding the tiny bell which was attached, so as to prevent it from tinkling. Once inside the yard, he walked stealthily to one of the side entrances and called out softly.

"Good morning," he called, noting with alarm that his voice did not sound at all like his own.

Immediately there was a reply, accompanied by the rustling sound of a kimono, and the next moment the old woman came to the door.

"Good morning, Mr. Fukiya," she greeted, kneeling and bowing politely. "I'm afraid your friend Mr. Saito isn't in."

"It's—it's you I wish to speak to," Fukiya explained quickly, "although the matter concerns Saito."

"Then please come in," she invited.

After he had taken off his shoes, she ushered him into the reception room, where she apologized for being alone in the house. "My maid is out today," she said, "so you must excuse me while I get the tea things. I won't be a minute." She rose and turned to leave the room.

This was the very opportunity Fukiya was waiting for. As the old woman bent herself a little in order to open the paper door, he pounced on her from behind and slowly proceeded to strangle her with his two gloved hands. Feebly, the old woman struggled, and one of her fingers scratched a folded screen which was standing close by.

After the old woman went limp, Fukiya carefully examined the damage. The screen had two folds and its surface was covered with gold flakes and a painting showing Komachi, a noted beauty of the feudal era. It was precisely on Komachi's face that the old woman had scratched in her death throes.

Fukiya soon recovered his composure, for he felt that this was too trivial to mean anything. He put the matter out of his mind and, going to the alcove, grabbed the pine tree by the trunk and pulled it out of the pot. As he had expected, he found a bundle lying in the base of the pot neatly wrapped up in oilpaper. Eagerly he undid the wrapping and grinned with satisfaction when a thick wad of paper money came to light.

Wasting no time, Fukiya took *half* of the money, stuffed it into the new purse that he took out of his pocket, re-wrapped the rest in the same oilpaper, and replaced the package at the bottom of the pot. He considered this move to be his master stroke, for he felt certain that it would throw the police miles off the track. Considering that the old woman was the only person who could have known exactly how much money she had hidden, no one would be any the wiser even if the amount were reduced to one half of the original sum.

Fukiya's next move was to stab the old woman carefully in the heart with the long jackknife. Then he wiped the blade on the woman's kimono and replaced it in his pocket. The purpose of this strange act was simply to make doubly sure that she could not be revived, a possibility he had often read about in crime novels. He had not killed her with the knife, for fear her blood might spatter on his clothing.

Fukiya replaced the tree in the pot, smoothed out the earth, and otherwise made certain that no clues had been left behind. Then he went out of the room. After closing the door, he tiptoed silently to the side entrance. Here, as he tied his shoelaces, he wondered if his shoes might leave tell-tale marks. But then he decided there was no danger, for the entryway was floored with cement. Stepping out into the garden, he felt even more secure, because it was a sunny day and the ground was hard and dry. Now, the only thing left for him to do was to walk to the front gate, open it, and vanish from the scene.

His heart was beating wildly, for he realized that one slip now would be fatal. He strained his ears for the slightest warning of danger, such as approaching footfalls, but all he could hear were the melodious notes of a Japanese harp tinkling in the distance. Straightening his shoulders, Fukiya strode to the gate, opened it boldly, and walked away.

Four or five blocks away from the old woman's house there stood a high, stone wall enclosing an old Shinto shrine. Fukiya dropped his jackknife and his blood-spattered gloves through a crevice in the wall down into a ditch, then walked on in a leisurely manner to a small park where he frequently went walking. Here he sat on a bench and casually watched several children playing on the swings.

After spending considerable time in the park, he rose from his seat, yawned and stretched, and then made his way to a nearby police station. Greeting the sergeant at the desk with a perfectly innocent look, he produced his well-filled purse.

"Officer, I just found this purse on the street. It's full of money, so I thought I'd better turn it in."

The policeman took the purse, examined its contents, and asked several routine questions. Fukiya, perfectly calm and self-possessed, answered straightforwardly, indicating the place and time he had made his "find." Naturally, all the information he gave was pure fabrication, with one exception: he gave his correct name and address.

After filling out several forms, the sergeant handed him a receipt. Fukiya pocketed the receipt, and for a moment wondered again if he was acting wisely. From every point of view, however, this was assuredly the safest course to take. Nobody knew that the old lady's money had been reduced by half. Also, it was quite obvious to Fukiya that no one would come to claim the purse. According to Japanese law, all the money in the purse would become his if no one claimed it within one year. Of course, it would be a long time to wait, but what of it? It was just like money in the bank—something he could count on, something to look forward to.

On the other hand, if he had hidden the money, to await an opportune time to spend it, it would have meant risking his neck every moment of the day. But the way he had chosen eliminated even the remotest danger of detection, even if the old lady had kept a record of the serial numbers of the banknotes.

While walking home from the police station Fukiya continued to gloat silently over the masterful way he had carried out his crime. "A simple case of sheer genius," he said to himself with a chuckle. "And what a big joke on the police. Imagine! A thief turning in his spoils! Under such circumstances, how could anyone possibly suspect me? Why, not even the Great Buddha himself would ever guess the truth!"

On the following day, after waking from a sound and untroubled sleep, Fukiya looked at the morning paper, delivered to his bedside by the maid of the boardinghouse. Stifling a yawn, he glanced at the page which carried the human-interest stories. Suddenly he caught sight of a brief item which caused his eyes to open wide. The first part of the story was an account of the discovery of the old woman's body. This was neither surprising nor startling to Fukiya. But the report went on to disclose that his friend Saito had been arrested by the police as the main suspect, having been discovered with a large sum of money on his person.

Actually, Fukiya thought, this fact too was nothing to become disturbed about. Instead, the development was decidedly advantageous to his own security. As one of Saito's closest friends, however, he also realized that he would have to inquire about him at the police station.

Fukiya dressed hastily and then called at the police station mentioned in the newspaper story. This turned out to be the very same place where he had reported the "finding" of the purse. "Curse my luck!" he swore to himself when he made this embarrassing discovery. Why hadn't he selected a different police station to report the money to? Well, it was too late now to change things.

Skilfully, he expressed deep anxiety over the unfortunate plight of his friend. He asked if they would permit him to see Saito and received a polite no. He then tried to make a few inquiries into the circumstances which had led to his friend's arrest, but here again he was refused.

Fukiya, however, didn't much care, for even without being told he could easily imagine what had happened. On the fateful day, Saito must have returned to the house ahead of the maid. By that time, of course, he himself had already committed his horrible deed and left the house. Then Saito must have found the corpse. Before reporting the crime to the police, however, he must have remembered the money hidden in the pot. If this was the work of a robber, Saito must have figured, the money would surely be gone. Curious to know if his reasoning was correct, he had examined the pot and had found the money there wrapped in oilpaper. And Fukiya could easily imagine what must have happened after that.

Undoubtedly Saito was tempted to keep the money for himself. This was a natural reaction, although, of course, it was a foolish thing for him to do. Thinking that everybody would believe that the murderer of the old woman had stolen the money, Saito pocketed the whole amount. And his next move? This, too, was easy to surmise. He had recklessly gone ahead and reported his discovery of the old woman's corpse, with the money still on his person, never suspecting that he would be one of the first to be questioned and searched. What an utter fool!

But wait, Fukiya reasoned further, Saito would certainly put up a desperate struggle to clear himself of suspicion. Then what? Would his statements possibly incriminate him, Fukiya, in any way? If Saito just kept insisting that the money was his, all might be well. But, then, the fact that the amount was exceptionally large—much too large for a student like Saito to possess—might give the lie to such a statement. The only alternative left for Saito would be to tell the truth—the whole truth. This would lead, by clever cross-examination on the part of the prosecutor, to the revelation that Saito had also told Fukiya where the old lady had hidden her money.

"Only two days preceding the day of the crime," Fukiya could even hear Saito telling the court, "my friend Fukiya conversed with the victim in the very room in which she was murdered. Knowing that she had that money hidden in the tree pot, could he not have committed the crime? I also wish to remind you, gentleman of the court, that Fukiya has always been notorious for being financially hard up!"

Although feeling decidedly uncomfortable after this soliloquy, Fukiya's optimism soon conquered his initial dismay. Emerging from the police station with a perfectly blank look on his face, he returned to his boardinghouse and ate a rather late breakfast. While eating, his original bravado returned, and he even made a point of telling the maid who served him about several aspects of the case.

Shortly after, he went to school, where he found, both on the campus and in the classrooms, that Saito's arrest as a suspect in the murder case was the main topic of conversation.

The investigator placed in charge of this sensational case was District Attorney Kasamori, noted not only as a man with excellent legal training, but also well known for valuable accomplishments of his own, especially in the field of psychological research. Whenever he came across a case which could not be unraveled by the standard methods of crime detection, he employed his fund of psychological knowledge with amazing results. With a man of Kasamori's reputation taking in hand the case of the old lady's murder, the public immediately became convinced that the mystery would soon be solved.

Kasamori too was confident that he could ultimately crack the case, no matter how complex it appeared at this early stage of the investigation. He began with a preliminary check of everything connected with the case, so that by the time it reached a public trial every single phase would be as clear as daylight. As the investigation proceeded, however, he found the case more and more difficult to handle. From the outset, the police kept insisting that no one but Saito could be the guilty party. Kasamori himself admitted the logic of the police theory, for, after all, every person who had been even remotely connected with the murdered old woman had been investigated and cleared of suspicion—everyone, that is, except her student lodger, the hapless Saito. Fukiya too had been among those who had been questioned, along with creditors of the old woman, her tenants, and even casual acquaintances, but he had quickly been eliminated.

In the case of Saito, there was one major point which worked to his great disadvantage. This was that he was extremely weak by nature and, completely terrorized by the stern atmosphere of the court, he was unable to answer even the simplest questions without first stuttering and stammering and showing all the symptoms of a man with a guilty conscience. Furthermore, in his excited state, he often retracted his previous statements, forgot vital details, and then tried to cover up by making other contradictory remarks, all of which tended only to incriminate him further and further. Simultaneously, there was another factor which tortured him and drove him to the verge of insanity. This was the fact that he *was* guilty of having stolen half of the old woman's money, precisely as Fukiya had theorized.

The district attorney carefully summed up the evidence, circumstantial as it was, against Saito, and pitied him deeply. It could not be denied that all the odds were against him. But, Kasamori asked himself again and again, had this weak, blubbering fool been capable of committing such a vicious, cold-blooded murder? He doubted it. So far Saito had not confessed, and conclusive proof of his guilt was still lacking.

A month went by, but the preliminary probe had not yet been completed. The district attorney became decidedly annoyed and impatient at the slow pace of the investigation.

"Curse the slow-grinding wheels of the law!" he exploded to a subordinate one day, while rechecking his documents on the case for what was probably the hundredth time. "At this rate, it'll take us a thousand years to solve the case." He then strode angrily to another desk and picked up a sheaf of routine documents filled out by the captain of the police station in whose jurisdiction the murder of the old lady fell. He looked casually at one of the papers and noticed that a purse containing ninety-five thousand yen in thousand-yen notes had been found at a spot near the old lady's house on the same day of the murder. The finder of the money, he further learned from the report, was a student, Fukiya by name, and a close friend of Saito's, the key murder suspect! For some reason— possibly because of the urgency of other duties—the police captain had failed to submit his report earlier.

After finishing reading the report, Kasamori's eyes lit up with a strange glow. For a full month now he had felt like a person fumbling in the dark. And then came this information, like a thin ray of light. Could it have any significance, any bearing on the case at hand? He decided to find out without delay.

Fukiya was quickly summoned, and the district attorney questioned him closely. After a full hour's questioning, however, Kasamori found he was getting nowhere. Asked as to why he had not mentioned the incident of his finding the purse when he had been interrogated previously in connection with the murder, Fukiya maintained calmly that he had not thought the matter to have any bearing on the case.

This reply, given straightforwardly, sounded most reasonable, for the money believed to have belonged to the old lady had been found in Saito's possession. Naturally, therefore, who could have imagined that the money found on the street was also a part of the old lady's property?

Nevertheless, Kasamori was deeply puzzled. Was it nothing but a mere coincidence that the very man who was a close friend of Saito's, the leading suspect, the man who, according to Saito's testimony in court, had also known where the old lady had hidden her money, had picked up so large a sum at a spot not far from the place where the murder had been committed? Here, indeed, was a conundrum worthy of the mind of a master sleuth.

Struggling angrily with the problem, the district attorney cursed the unfortunate fact that the serial numbers of the banknotes had not been recorded by the old woman. Had they been recorded, it would have been a most simple task to verify whether the money found by Fukiya was part of the same loot.

"If only I could find one single clue," he kept repeating to himself.

In the days that followed, Kasamori revisited the scene of the crime and talked to the victim's relatives, going over the same ground again and again, but all to no avail. He had to admit that he was up against a wall, with not a single tangible clue to follow up.

So far as he could see, the only possible way in which he could explain the episode of Fukiya's finding the purse was that the man had stolen half of the old lady's savings, left the remainder in the hiding place, put the stolen money in a purse, and pretended that he had found it on the street. But was it really possible that such a fantastic thing could have been done? The purse, of course, had been subjected to the closest scrutiny and placed under a micro-scope for even the faintest of possible clues, but all these efforts had proved negative. Also, according to Fukiya's own statement, he had taken a walk on the day of the murder; in fact, he had even admitted that he had passed the old lady's house. Would a man who was guilty be so bold as to make such a dangerous admission? And then, what about the weapon which had been used to stab the old woman? The entire house and garden as well as the surrounding area within a large radius had been searched with a fine-tooth comb, but there was not a trace of it.

In the absence of conclusive evidence to the contrary, Kasamori felt that the police were justified in pointing to Saito as the most likely suspect. But then again, the district attorney reasoned, if Saito could be guilty, so could Fukiya! Thus, after an investigation which had stretched out to a full month and a half, the only point which had been established was that there were two possible suspects, but without a shred of concrete evidence to convict either.

Reaching this impasse, Kasamori decided there was still one other method he could use in his attempt to break the case. This was to subject the two suspects to a psychological test—a method which had been used in the past.

When he had first been questioned by the police, two or three days after the murder, Fukiya had learned that the district attorney who had been put in charge of the case was the noted amateur psychologist Kasamori, and the information filled him with panic. Cool and collected as he had been until then, he soon came to dread the very sound of the district attorney's name, especially after he had been summoned a second time and questioned by Kasamori himself. Supposing, just supposing, he were to be subjected to a psychological test. What then? Would he be able to hold his own in the face of such an experiment, the nature of which he knew absolutely nothing about?

The shock of this possibility was so stunning that he became too uneasy to attend his classes. He remained in his room, on the pretext of illness, and tried desperately to figure out how he could match wits for wits. Of course, there was absolutely no way of anticipating the form of psychological test that Kasamori might employ. Fukiya, therefore, applied all the test methods he could possibly imagine on himself in order to discover the best possible way to circumvent them. Since a psychological test, by nature, was a method applied to reveal all false statements, Fukiya's first thought was that it would be utterly impossible to lie his way out of such a test.

Fukiya knew there were psychological tests which used lie-detector devices to record physical reactions. He had also heard that there was a simpler method which used a stop watch to measure the time it took a suspect to answer questions. Reflecting upon the many and various psychological methods of crime detection, Fukiya became more and more concerned. Supposing he were caught by a surprise question like "You're the one who killed the old woman, aren't you?" fired at him point-blank? Fukiya felt confident that he would be able to shoot back calmly: "What proof do you have for such a wild supposition?" But if a lie detector were to be used, wouldn't it record his startled state of mind? Wouldn't it be absolutely impossible for a normal human being to prevent such physical reactions?

Fukiya tried asking himself various hypothetical questions. Strangely, no matter how unexpected his questions were, when they were addressed *to himself by himself*, he could not imagine that they produced any physical changes within him. Gradually he became convinced that so long as he avoided becoming nervously excited, he would be safe even in the face of the most accurate instrument.

While conducting these various experiments on himself, Fukiya suddenly became convinced that the effects of a psychological test might be neutralized by training. He became sure that the reaction of a man's nerves to a pointed question would become less each time the question was repeated. Granting that his reasoning was sound, Fukiya told himself, the best method of neutralization was to become accustomed to the questions. He reasoned that his own questions to himself produced no reaction because he already knew both question and answer before he spoke.

Fukiya painstakingly began to examine every page of a thick dictionary and to jot down those words which might possibly be used in questions to be thrown at him. For a full week he spent most of his waking hours this way, training his nerves against all possible questions. Then, feeling that his mind had been fairly well fortified in this field, he turned to another. This was the word-association test, which Fukiya knew psychiatrists used widely in examining patients.

As Fukiya understood it, the patient—or accused—would be told to answer any word given him with the first word that came to his mind, and then the examiner would call off a list of words with absolutely no bearing on the case—"screen," "desk," "ink," "pen," and the like. The significance of the test lay in the fact that the word given in reply would have some mental association with the previously recited word. For example, if the word happened to be "screen," the culprit might come out with such words as "window," "window sill," "paper," or "door." And in the course of the test such incriminating words as "knife," "money," or "purse" would be slipped in so as to befuddle the accused in his association of ideas.

In Fukiya's case, for instance, if he were not on his guard, he might reply "money" to "dwarf tree," thereby unconsciously admitting that he knew money to have been stolen from the pot of the tree. On the other hand, if he prepared for the ordeal in advance, he could answer with a harmless word like "earthenware" instead of "money." Then, of course, he would be in the clear.

Fukiya knew that, in conducting the "word diagnosis," the exact time elapsing between question and answer was always recorded. If, for example, the accused said "door" in reply to "screen" in one second and then took three seconds to say "earthenware" in reply to "dwarf tree," it could be inferred that the man had taken more time to frame the second reply in order to suppress the first idea which leaped to his mind. Such a time discrepancy, of course, would arouse suspicion.

Fukiya also reasoned that if he were given a word test, it would be far safer to answer in the most obviously natural manner. He, therefore, decided that in reply to "dwarf tree" he would say either "pine" or "money" because, even if he had not been the culprit, the police would know that he would be sufficiently acquainted with the facts of the crime for this to be a natural answer for him to give. One question, however, called for deeper thought. This was the matter of timing. But he felt that this too could be managed by careful training. The important thing was that if a word like "dwarf tree" was fired at him, he should be able to reply "money" or "pine" without a moment's hesitation.

For several days Fukiya worked hard at training himself, until finally he felt that he could satisfactorily pass the strictest test. Furthermore, he derived immense consolation from the knowledge that Saito, although innocent of the murder, would also be exposed to the same volley of questions, and would certainly exhibit a similar degree of nervousness.

The more Fukiya considered all these possibilities, the greater became his sense of security and self-confidence. In fact, now that he was once again feeling completely at ease, he was able to whistle and sing, and even to wish strongly for a summons from District Attorney Kasamori.

It was the day after the district attorney had subjected both suspects to psychological tests, and Kasamori was in his study at home, busily going over the results of the tests. Suddenly his maid announced that he had a visitor.

Literally buried under his papers, the district attorney was in no mood to play host, so he growled impatiently to his servant: "Kindly tell whoever it is that I'm too busy to see anyone today."

"Yes, sir," the maid replied obediently, but as she turned, the door suddenly opened, and the caller popped his head in playfully.

"Good afternoon, Mr. District Attorney," the caller said cheerfully, ignoring the startled look of the servant. "Don't tell me you're too busy even to see your old friend Akechi."

Kasamori dropped his pince-nez and looked up sharply. But immediately his face broadened into a happy grin.

"Why, hello, Dr. Akechi," he replied. "I didn't know it was you. Forgive me. Step right in and make yourself comfortable. As a matter of fact, I was hoping you'd drop in."

Kasamori dismissed the maid with a grunt and motioned to his guest to be seated. A sleuth with a mind keen as a razor and a unique technique for solving knotty problems, Dr. Kogoro Akechi was the one man whom the district attorney would have stopped to talk to even if he had been on his way to catch a train. On several previous occasions he had asked for Dr. Akechi's cooperation in cracking what had been labeled "impossible cases," and in every instance the man had lived up to his reputation as one of Japan's most remarkable detectives.

After lighting a cigarette, Dr. Akechi nodded meaningfully toward the stacks of papers on the district attorney's desk.

"I see you're very busy," he remarked casually. "Is it the case of the old woman who was murdered recently?"

"Yes," the district attorney replied. "Frankly, I'm at the end of my rope."

"Pessimism doesn't become you, Mr. District Attorney," said Dr. Akechi with a dry laugh. "Come, now, tell me the results of the psychological tests you gave your two suspects."

Kasamori raised his eyebrows. "How the devil did you know about my tests?" he asked sharply.

"One of your assistants told me," Dr. Akechi explained. "You see, I'm deeply interested in the case too, so I thought I'd come and offer you my humble services."

"It was kind of you to come," Kasamori replied gratefully and quickly launched into a discussion of his complicated experiments.

"The results, as you will notice," he said, "are clear enough, but there is something that has me completely baffled. Yesterday I gave each suspect two tests, a lie-detector test based on pulse measurements and a word-association test. In Fukiya's case the pulse measurements were almost always above suspicion. But when I compared the results of the word-association test, I found a tremendous difference between Saito and Fukiya. In fact, the results were so far apart that I must admit I'm completely at a loss for an explanation. Just look at this questionnaire and observe the differences in the time taken by the two suspects in their replies to the same words."

Kasamori then handed Dr. Akechi the following tabulation of the results of the word-association test:

| WORD GIVEN | FUKIYA | | SAITO | |
|---|---|---|---|---|
| | Answer | Time Taken | Answer | Time Taken |
| head | hair | 0.9 sec. | tail | 1.2 sec. |
| green | grass | 0.7 " | grass | 1.1 " |
| water | hot water | 0.9 " | fish | 1.3 " |
| sing | songs | 1.1 " | geisha | 1.5 " |
| long | short | 1.0 " | cord | 1.2 " |
| *kill | knife | 0.8 " | crime | 3.1 " |
| boat | river | 0.9 " | water | 2.2 " |
| window | door | 0.8 " | glass | 1.5 " |
| food | beefsteak | 1.0 " | fish | 1.3 " |
| *money | bank notes | 0.7 " | bank | 3.5 " |
| cold | water | 1.1 " | winter | 3.2 " |
| illness | cold | 1.6 " | tuberculosis | 2.3 " |
| needle | thread | 1.0 " | thread | 1.2 " |
| *pine | dwarf tree | 0.8 " | tree | 2.3 " |
| mountain | high | 0.9 " | river | 1.4 " |
| *blood | flowing | 1.0 " | red | 3.9 " |
| new | old | 0.8 " | dress | 3.0 " |
| hate | spider | 1.2 " | sickness | 1.5 " |
| *dwarf tree | pine | 0.6 " | flower | 6.2 " |
| bird | flying | 0.9 " | canary | 3.6 " |
| book | library | 1.0 " | novel | 1.3 " |
| *oilpaper | conceal | 1.0 " | parcel | 4.0 " |
| friend | Saito | 1.1 " | Fukiya | 1.8 " |
| box | wood | 1.0 " | doll | 1.2 " |
| *crime | murder | 0.7 " | police | 3.7 " |
| woman | lover | 1.0 " | sister | 1.3 " |
| painting | screen | 0.9 " | landscape | 1.3 " |
| *steal | money | 0.7 " | necklace | 4.1 " |
| Note: | Words marked with an asterisk (*) are directly related to the crime. | | | |

"You see, everything is very plain," said the district attorney after Dr. Akechi had examined the paper. "According to this, Saito must have wilfully resorted to trickery. This is evident from the fact that he took so much time to respond, not only to the incriminating words, but also the unimportant dummy words. Also, the long time he took in replying to 'dwarf tree' probably indicates he was trying to suppress such natural, but in his opinion incriminating, words as 'money' or 'pine.' Now, on the other hand, take the case of Fukiya. He said 'pine' in reply to 'dwarf tree,' 'conceal' in reply to 'oilpaper,' and 'murder' in reply to 'crime.' Surely, if he were really guilty, he would have avoided uttering those words. Yet he replied in a perfectly matter-of-fact tone, without the slightest hesitation. From these facts, therefore, I am strongly inclined to rule him out as a suspect. At the same time, however, when it comes to deciding positively that Saito is the guilty man, I simply can't bring myself to it, despite this record."

Dr. Akechi listened calmly to the district attorney's reasoning without making any effort to interrupt. But after the latter had concluded his summing up, Dr. Akechi's eyes gleamed brightly, and he began to speak.

"Have you ever stopped to consider the weak points of a psychological test?" he began. "De Quiros has stated, in criticism of the views entertained by Muensterberg, who advocated the psychological test, that although the system was devised as a substitute for torture, its actual result might well incriminate the innocent just as much as had trial by torture, thus allowing the real criminal to escape. Muensterberg himself has stated in his books that a psychological test is definitely effective in verifying whether a suspected person knows a certain other person, or place, or thing, but that for other purposes it is very dangerous. I realize that my telling you all this, Kasamori, is decidedly superfluous, but I just wanted to call your attention to these vital facts."

The district attorney replied, with a trace of annoyance in his voice, that he was aware of these facts.

"Well, then," Dr. Akechi continued, "let us study the case at hand from an entirely different angle. Supposing—just supposing—an innocent man who is extremely nervous is suspected of a crime. He is arrested at the scene of the crime and is, therefore, aware of all the circumstances and the macabre setting. In such an event could he preserve his composure if he was subjected to a rigid psychological test? He might very naturally say to himself: 'They are going to test me. What shall I say to escape suspicion?' Considering that his mind would naturally be greatly excited, would not a psychological test conducted under such circumstances tend to incriminate the innocent party, as De Quiros has mentioned?"

"I suppose you are talking about Saito," said the district attorney, still annoyed.

"Yes," Dr. Akechi replied. "And now, granting that my reasoning is sound, he would be entirely innocent of the murder, although of course, the possibility still remains that he might actually have stolen the money. And now comes the big question: Who killed the old woman?"

Kasamori interrupted abruptly at this point. "Come now, Dr. Akechi," he said impatiently. "Don't keep me in suspense. Have you come to any definite conclusion as to who the actual killer is?"

"Yes, I think so," Dr. Akechi replied, smiling broadly. "Judging by the results of your psychological tests, I believe Fukiya is our man, although, of course, I cannot swear to it yet. Could we have him brought here? If I can ask him a few more questions, I feel positive that I can get to the bottom of this most intriguing case."

"But what about evidence?" the district attorney asked, taken aback by the other's cool manner. "Just *how* are you going to get your proof?"

"Give a guilty man enough rope," rejoined Dr. Akechi philosophically, "and he'll supply enough evidence to hang himself."

Dr. Akechi then outlined his theory in detail. After hearing it, Kasamori clapped his hands to call his servant. Then, taking up pen and paper from his desk, he wrote the following note, addressed to Fukiya:

*Your friend Saito has been found guilty of the crime. As there are a few points I wish to discuss with you, I request you to call at my private residence immediately.*

He signed the message and handed it to the servant.

\*    \*    \*

Fukiya had just returned from school when he received the note. Unaware that it was the bait for a carefully laid trap, he was elated over the news. Without bothering even to have his supper, he hurried to the district attorney's house.

As soon as Fukiya entered the study, District Attorney Kasamori greeted him warmly and invited him to sit down.

"I owe you an apology, Mr. Fukiya," he said, "for having suspected you for so long. Now that I know you to be innocent, I thought you might like to hear a few of the circumstances surrounding your complete exoneration."

The district attorney ordered refreshments for everybody and then ceremoniously introduced the student to Dr. Akechi, although he used quite a different name for the latter.

"Mr. Yamamoto," he explained, indicating Dr. Akechi without batting an eyelash, "is a lawyer who has been appointed by the old woman's heirs to settle her estate."

After refreshments of tea and rice-cakes, they discussed various unimportant matters, Fukiya talking very freely. In fact, as the time quickly sped by, he became the most loquacious of the three. Suddenly, however, he glanced at his wrist watch and rose abruptly.

"I didn't realize that it was so late," he announced apologetically. "If you'll forgive me, I think I'd better be leaving."

"Of course, of course," said the district attorney drily.

Dr. Akechi, however, suddenly interrupted. "One moment, please," he said to Fukiya. "There is just one trivial question I'd like to ask you before you leave. I wonder if you know there was a two-fold gold screen standing in the room where the old woman was murdered? It has been slightly damaged, and a minor legal issue has been raised over it. You see, it appears that the screen didn't belong to the old woman, but was being held by her as security for a loan. And now the owner has come forward with the demand that he be reimbursed for the damage. My clients, however, are reluctant to agree to this, for they contend that the screen might have been damaged *before* it was brought into the house. Really, of course, it's a very trivial matter, but if you could by any chance help me to clear it up, I would be more than grateful. The reason I'm asking is because I understand you frequently visited the house to see your friend Saito. Perhaps you may have noticed the screen. Saito, of course, was asked about it, but in his excited condition nothing that he said seemed to make much sense. I also tried to contact the old lady's maid, but she's already returned to her home in the country, and I haven't yet had an opportunity to write to her."

Although Dr. Akechi had mentioned all this in a perfectly matter-of-fact tone of voice, Fukiya felt a slight tremor in his heart. But he quickly reassured himself: "Why should I be startled? The case is already closed." He then asked himself what answer he should make. After a brief pause he decided that his best course would be to speak frankly, just as he had always done.

"As the district attorney knows," he began, smiling innocently, "I went into the room on only one occasion. That was two days before the murder. However, now that I come to think of it, I do remember that screen distinctly, and I can say that, when I saw it, it was *not* damaged."

"Are you absolutely sure of this?" Dr. Akechi quickly asked. "Remember now, the damage I mean is a scratch on the face of Komachi painted on the screen."

"Yes, yes, I know," Fukiya said emphatically. "And I'm positive, I tell you, that there was no scratch, neither on the face of the beautiful Komachi nor anywhere else. If it had been damaged in any way, I'm sure I could not have failed to notice it."

"Well, then, would you mind making an affidavit?" Dr. Akechi shot back. "You see, the owner of the screen is very insistent in his demand, and I find it very difficult to deal with him."

"Not at all," Fukiya said, in his most cooperative tone. "I would be most willing to make an affidavit any time you say."

Dr. Akechi thanked the student with a smile, then scratched his head, a habit of his whenever he was excited. "And now," he continued, "I think you can admit that you know a great deal about the screen, because in the record of your psychological test, I noticed that you replied 'screen' to 'picture.' A screen, as you know, is something rare in a student boardinghouse."

Fukiya was surprised at Dr. Akechi's new tone. He wondered what the devil the man was trying to get at.

Again the man who had been introduced as a lawyer addressed him. "By the way," he said, "there was still another point which came to my attention. When the psychological test was conducted yesterday, there were eight highly significant danger words on the list. You, of course, passed the test without a hitch. In fact, in my opinion, it went off altogether *too* smoothly. With your permission I'd like to have you take a look at your record on those eight key words."

Dr. Akechi produced the tabulation of the results and said: "You took little less time to answer the key words than the insignificant words. For example, in answer to 'dwarf tree,' you said 'pine' in only six-tenths of a second. This indicates remarkable innocence. Note that you took one-tenth of a second longer to answer to the word 'green,' which of all the twenty-eight words on the list is generally the easiest to respond to."

Not quite understanding Dr. Akechi's motive, Fukiya began to wonder where all this talk was leading. Just what was this talkative lawyer up to, anyway, he asked himself with a shudder. He had to know, and quickly, for it might be a trap.

"'Dwarf tree,' 'oilpaper,' 'crime,' or any other of the eight key words are not nearly so easy to associate with other words as are such words as 'head' or 'green,'" Dr. Akechi continued tenaciously. "And yet, you managed to answer the difficult words quicker than the easier ones. What does it all mean? This is what puzzled me all along. But now, let me try to guess exactly what was in your mind. Really, you know, it might prove to be quite amusing. Of course, if I'm wrong, I humbly beg your pardon."

Fukiya felt a cold shiver run down his spine. This weird business was now really beginning to prey on his nerves. But before he could even attempt to interrupt, Dr. Akechi began speaking again.

"Surely you have been well aware all along of the dangers of a psychological test," he insisted to Fukiya. "I take it, therefore, that you prepared yourself for the test well in advance. For example, for all words associated with the crime, you carefully drafted ready-made replies, so that you could recite them at a moment's notice. Now, please don't misunderstand, Mr. Fukiya. I am not trying to criticize the method you adopted. I only want to point out that a psychological test is a dangerous experiment on occasions. More often than not, it snares the innocent, and frees the guilty."

Dr. Akechi paused to let the hidden implications of his statements sink in, then he resumed again.

"You, Mr. Fukiya, made the fatal mistake of making your preparations with too much cunning. When you were confronted with the test, you spoke too fast. This, of course, was only natural, because you were afraid that if you took too much time in answering the questions, you would be suspected. But . . . you overdid it!"

Dr. Akechi paused again, noting with grim satisfaction that Fukiya's face was turning a sickly grey. Then he continued his summation:

"I come now to another significant phase of the test. Why did you choose to reply with such words as 'money,' 'conceal,' and 'murder'—all words which were liable to incriminate you? I will tell you. It was because you purposely wanted to make out that you were naive. Am I not right, Fukiya? Isn't my reasoning sound?"

Fukiya stared with glassy eyes at the face of his tormentor. He tried hard to look away, to evade the cold, accusing eyes of Dr. Akechi; but for some reason he found he couldn't. It appeared to Kasamori as though Fukiya had been caught in a hypnotic trance and was unable to manifest any emotion other than fear.

"This seeming innocence of yours," Dr. Akechi continued, "just did not strike me as being truly genuine. So I thought up the idea of asking you about the gold screen. Of course, the answer you gave was exactly the one I anticipated."

Dr. Akechi suddenly turned to the district attorney. "Now, I want to ask you a simple question, Mr. District Attorney. Just *when* was the screen brought into the house of the old woman?"

"The day before the crime, on the fourth of last month," Kasamori replied.

"*The day before the crime*, did you say?" Dr. Akechi repeated loudly. "But that's very strange. Mr. Fukiya just stated a moment ago that he saw it *two days before* the crime was committed, which was the third of last month. Furthermore, he was very positive as to where he had seen it—in the very room where the old woman was murdered! Now, this is all very contradictory. Surely, one of you two must be mistaken!"

"Mr. Fukiya must be the one who has made the miscalculation," observed the district attorney with a sly grin. "Until the afternoon of the fourth the screen was at the house of the owner. There is no question about it!"

Dr. Akechi watched Fukiya's face with rapt interest, for the expression that the latter now wore was akin to that of a little girl on the verge of tears.

Suddenly Dr. Akechi pointed an accusing finger at the student, and demanded sharply: "Why did you say you saw something which you could not have seen? It's really too bad that you had to remember the classical painting, because by doing so you have betrayed yourself! In your anxiety to pretend to tell the truth, you even tried to elaborate on the details. Isn't this so, Fukiya? Could you have noticed that there was no folding screen in the room when you entered it two days before the crime? No, you certainly would not have paid any attention to such a detail, because it had nothing to do with your plans. Furthermore, I think that even if it had been there, it would not have attracted your attention, because the room was elaborately decorated with various other paintings and antiques of a similar nature. So it was quite natural for you to assume that the screen which you saw on the day of the crime must have been there two days previously. My questions bewildered you, so you accepted their implications. Now, had you been an ordinary criminal, you would not have answered as you did. You would have tried to deny knowing anything about anything. But I had you sized up from the very beginning as being a real intellectual, and as such, I knew you would try to be as outspoken as possible so long as you did not touch upon anything dangerous. But I anticipated your moves, and played my hand accordingly."

Dr. Akechi then broke out into loud, boisterous laughter. "Too bad," he said sarcastically to the crestfallen Fukiya, "that you had to be trapped by a humble lawyer like myself."

Fukiya remained silent, knowing that it would be useless to try and talk his way out. Clever as he was, he realized that any attempt to correct the fatal slip he had made would only drag him deeper and deeper into the pit of doom.

After a long silence, Dr. Akechi spoke again. "Can you hear the scratching of pen against paper, Fukiya? A police stenographer in the next room has been recording everything we've said here."

He called out to someone in the adjoining room, and a moment later a young stenographer entered the study, carrying a sheaf of papers.

"Please read your notes," Dr. Akechi requested.

The stenographer read the complete record, taken down word for word.

"Now, Mr. Fukiya," Dr. Akechi said, "I would appreciate it if you will kindly sign the document, and seal it with your fingerprint. Certainly you can have no objection, for you promised to testify regarding the screen at any time."

Meekly, Fukiya signed the record and sealed it with an imprint of his thumb. A few moments later, several detectives from police headquarters, summoned by the district attorney, led the confessed slayer away.

The show now over, Dr. Akechi turned to the district attorney. "As I have remarked before," he said, "Muensterberg was right when he said that the true merit of a psychological test lies in the discovery of whether or not a suspected person noticed any other person, or thing, at a certain place. In Fukiya's case, everything hinged on whether or not he had seen the screen. Apart from establishing that fact, no psychological test that you might have given Fukiya would have brought any remarkable results. Being the intellectual scoundrel he is, his mind was too well prepared to be defeated by any routine psychological questions."

Rising from his seat with the air of a professor leaving his class following a lengthy lecture, Dr. Akechi put on his hat, then paused briefly for a final statement.

"Just one more thing I would like to mention," he said with a smile. "In conducting a psychological test, there is no need for strange charts, machines, or word games. As discovered by the famous Judge Ooka, in the colorful days of eighteenth-century

Tokyo, who frequently applied psychological tests based on mere questions and answers, it's not too difficult to catch criminals in psychological traps. But of course, you have to ask the right questions. Well, good night, Mr. District Attorney. And thanks for the refreshments."

# The Red Chamber

## by EDOGAWA RAMPO

### TRANSLATED BY JAMES B. HARRIS

The seven grave men, including myself, had gathered as usual to exchange blood-curdling horror stories. We sank into the deep armchairs, covered with scarlet velvet, in the room which had been dubbed the "Red Chamber" and waited eagerly for the narrator of the evening to begin his tale.

In the center of the group was a large, round table, also covered with scarlet velvet, and on it was a carved bronze candelabrum in which three large candles burned with flickering flames. On all sides of the room—even over the doors and windows—heavy red-silk curtains hung in graceful folds from ceiling to floor. The flames of the candles cast monstrously enlarged shadows of the secret society of seven on the curtains in hues dark like that of blood. Rising and falling, expanding and contracting, the seven silhouettes crept among the curves of the crimson drapery like horrible insects.

In this chamber I always felt as though I were sitting in the belly of some enormous, prehistoric beast, and thought I could even feel its heart beat in a slow tempo appropriate to its hugeness.

For a while all of us remained silent. As I sat with the rest like one bewitched, I unconsciously stared at the dark-red shadowy faces around the table and shuddered. Although I was perfectly familiar with the features of the others, I always felt chills creep down my spine whenever I studied them at close hand, for they all seemed perpetually unexpressive and motionless, like Japanese Noh masks.

At last, Tanaka, who had only recently been initiated into the society, cleared his throat to speak. He sat poised on the edge of his chair, gazing at the candle flames. I happened to glance at his chin, but what I saw seemed more like a square block of bone—without flesh or skin—and his whole face was akin to that of an ugly marionette strangely come alive.

"Having been admitted to the society as an accredited member," Tanaka suddenly began without any introduction, "I shall now proceed to contribute my first tale of horror."

As none of us made any move or comment, he quickly launched forth into his narrative:

I believe [he said] that I am in my right mind and that all my friends will vouch for my sanity, but whether I am really mentally fit or not, I will leave to you to judge. Yes, I may be mad! Or perhaps I may just be a mild neurotic case. But, at any rate, I must explain that I have always been weary of life . . . and to me the normal man's daily routine is—and always will be—a hateful boredom.

At first I gave myself up to various dissipations to distract my mind, but unfortunately, nothing seemed to relieve my profound boredom. Instead, everything I did only seemed to increase my disappointment the more. Constantly I kept asking myself: Is there no amusement left in the world for me? Am I doomed to die of yawning? Gradually I fell into a state of lethargy from which there seemed to be no escape. Nothing that I did—absolutely nothing—

succeeded in pleasing my fancy. Every day I took three meals, and when the evening shadows fell I went to bed. Slowly I began to feel that I was going stark raving mad. Eating and sleeping, eating and sleeping—just like a hog.

If my circumstances had required that I hustle for my daily living, perhaps my constant boredom would have been relieved. But such was not my luck. By this I do not mean to imply that I was born fabulously rich. If this had been the case, then again there might have been a solution to my problem, for certainly money would have brought me thrills in plenty—orgies in luxurious living, eccentric debaucheries, or even bloody sports as in the days of Nero and the gladiators—so long as I could pay the price. But, curse my luck, I was neither destitute nor rich, just comfortably well-off, with funds sufficient to ensure only an average standard of living.

To any ordinary audience I would at this point enlarge upon the tortures of a life of boredom. But to you gentlemen of the Red Chamber Society I know this is unnecessary. Assuredly it was for the very purpose of banishing the specter of boredom that has haunted you, as it has me, that you formed this society. Therefore I will not digress but continue with my story.

At all times, as I have stated, I wrestled with the all-absorbing question: How am I to amuse myself? On some occasions I toyed with the idea of becoming a detective and finding amusement in tracking down criminals. At other times I pondered the possibilities of psychic experiments, or even of eroticism. How about producing obscene motion pictures? Or better still, how about private pornographic stage productions with prostitutes and sexual maniacs for the cast? Other ideas which occurred to me were visits to lunatic asylums and prisons or, if permission could be gotten, the witnessing of executions. But for one reason or another none of these ideas appealed to me very strongly. To put it another way they seemed like a soft drink offered to a dipsomaniac who is thirsting for gin and absinthe, cognac and vodka, all in one glass. Yes, that was what I needed—a good stiff drink of amusement—real soul-satisfying amusement.

Suddenly, just when I was about to conclude that I would never find a solution to my problem, an idea struck me—a horrible idea.

At first I tried to shake it from me, for indeed my mind was now wading through treacherous swamps, and I knew I would be doomed if I did not check my impulses. And yet, the idea seemed to hold for me a peculiar fascination which I had never hitherto experienced. In short, gentlemen, the idea was . . . murder! Yes, here at last was an idea that seemed more worthy of a man of my character, a man willing to go to any lengths for a real thrill.

Finally, after convincing myself that I would never find peace of mind until I had committed a few murders, I carefully began to put some devilish plans into operation, just for the sheer pleasure of satisfying my lust for distraction. And now, at this point, before I proceed further, permit me to confess that, since that day when I first decided to become a murderer, I have been responsible for the deaths of nearly a hundred men, women, and children! Yes, almost a hundred innocent lives sacrificed on the altar of my eccentricity!

You might have inferred that I am now repentant for all the ghastly crimes I have committed. Well, that is definitely not the case. To tell the truth, I am not penitent at all. Far from it, for the fact of the matter is I have no conscience! So, instead of being racked with remorse, as apparently would any normal person, I simply became tired even of the bloody stimulus of murder. Again seeking some new diversion, I next took up the vice of opium-smoking. Gradually I became addicted to the drug, and today I can no longer do without a pipe at regular intervals.

So far, gentlemen, I have merely outlined the circumstances of my past—the murder of nearly a hundred people, all as yet undetected. I know, however, that the Supreme Judge who will pass sentence upon me for all my crimes is already demanding that I enter the portals of eternity, to roast in hellfire.

Now I shall relate the various events that made up my premeditated festival of crime. I do not doubt even for a moment that, when you have heard all the gruesome details, you will consider me a worthy member of your mystic society!

It all began about three years ago. In those days, as I have already told you, I was tired of every normal pastime and idled away my time with nothing whatever to do. In the spring of the year—as it was still very cold, it must have been about the end of February or the beginning of March—I had a strange experience one evening, the very incident that led me to take nearly one hundred lives.

I had been out late somewhere and, if I remember correctly, was a little tipsy. The time was about one in the morning. As I walked at a leisurely pace toward home, I suddenly came upon a man who seemed to be in a state of great confusion. I was startled when we almost collided, but he seemed to be even more frightened, for he stopped in his tracks, trembling. After a moment he peered into my face in the dim light of a street lamp and, to my great surprise, suddenly spoke.

"Does any doctor live hereabouts?" he asked.

"Yes," I immediately replied and asked what had happened.

The man hastily explained that he was a chauffeur and that he had accidentally run down and injured an old man who appeared to be a vagrant, some distance down the road. When he pointed out where the accident had occurred, I realized that it was in the very neighborhood of my house.

"Go to the left for a couple of blocks," I directed, "and you will find a house with a red lamp on the left-hand side. That's the office of Dr. Matsui. You'd better go there."

A few moments later I saw the chauffeur carrying the badly injured man to the house I had indicated. For some reason I kept watching until their dim figures vanished into the darkness. As I thought it inadvisable to interfere in such an affair, I returned to my bachelor quarters and promptly sank into the bed which had been prepared by my old housekeeper. Soon the alcohol in my system had me deep in sleep.

If, with the coming of sleep, I had forgotten all about that accident, it would have been the end of the affair. When I woke up the next morning, however, I remembered every detail of the previous night's episode. I began to wonder if the man who had been run down had succumbed to his injuries or had survived. Then suddenly something came to my mind with a jolt. Due to some strange quirk of the mind, or possibly because of the wine I had drunk, I had made a serious error in the directions I had given the chauffeur.

I was amazed. However drunk I might have been, I had surely not been out of my mind. Then why had I instructed the driver of the car to carry the unconscious man to the office of Dr. Matsui?

"Go to the left for a couple of blocks and you'll find a house with a red lamp on the left-hand side . . ." I remembered every word I had uttered. Why, why, hadn't I instructed the man to go to the right for one block and seek the aid of Dr. Kato, a well-known surgeon? Matsui, the doctor whom I had recommended to the chauffeur, was a notorious quack, utterly without experience in surgery. On the other hand, Dr. Kato was a brilliant surgeon. As I had known this all along, how, I kept asking myself, had I ever come to make such a silly mistake?

I began to feel more and more anxious over my blunder and sent my old housekeeper to make a few discreet inquiries among the neighbors. When she returned from her mission I learned that the worst had happened. Dr. Matsui had failed miserably in his surgical efforts, and the victim of the accident had died without recovering consciousness. According to the gossip of the neighbors, when the injured man was carried into the office of Dr. Matsui, the latter made no mention of the fact that he was a novice in surgery. If, even at that eleventh hour, he had directed the chauffeur to take the man to Dr. Kato, the unfortunate man might still have been saved. But, no! Rashly, he had worked on the man himself, and had failed.

When I learned these tragic facts, all my blood seemed to drain out of my body. Who had actually been responsible for the death of the poor old man, I asked myself. Of course, the chauffeur and Dr. Matsui had their share of the responsibility. And if someone had to be punished, the guardians of the law would certainly pick the chauffeur. And yet, wasn't it *I* who had really been the most responsible? If I had not made the fatal error of indicating the wrong doctor, that old man might have been saved! The chauffeur had only injured the victim . . . he had not killed him outright. As for Dr. Matsui, his failure was attributable only to his lack of surgical skill, and to no other cause. But I—I had been criminally negligent and had pronounced the death sentence on an innocent man.

Actually, of course, I was innocent, for I had only committed a blunder. But then, I asked myself, what if I had *purposely* given the wrong directions? Needless to say, in that case I would have been guilty of murder! And yet, even if the law were to punish the chauffeur, not the slightest suspicion would have fallen on me—the real murderer! Besides, even if I had been suspected in some way, could they have hanged me if I had testified in court that because I had been in a state of intoxication I had forgotten all about Dr. Kato, the good surgeon? All these thoughts raised a fascinating problem.

Gentlemen, have you ever theorized on murder along these lines? I myself thought of it for the first time only after the experience I have just related. If you ponder deeply on the matter, you will find that the world is indeed a dangerous place. Who knows when you yourselves may be directed to the wrong doctor—*intentionally, criminally*—by a man like myself?

To prove my theory I will outline another example of how a perfect crime can be perpetrated without the slightest danger of suspicion. Supposing, one day, you notice an old country woman crossing a downtown street, just about to put one foot down on the rails of the streetcar line. The traffic, we will also suppose, is heavy with motorcars, bicycles, and carts. Under these circumstances you would perceive the old woman is jittery, as is natural for a rustic in a big city. Suppose, now, that at the very moment she puts her foot on the rail a streetcar comes rushing down the tracks toward her. If the old woman does not notice the car and continues across the tracks, nothing will happen. But if someone should happen to shout "Look out, old woman!" what would be her natural reaction? It is superfluous for me to explain that she would suddenly become flustered and would pause to decide whether to go on or to step back. Now, if the motorman of the streetcar could not apply his brakes in time, the mere words "Look out, old woman!" would be as dangerous a weapon as any knife or firearm. I once successfully killed an old country woman in this way—but more of that later.

[Tanaka paused a moment, and a hideous grin contorted his flushed face. Then he continued.]

Yes, in such a case the man who sounds the warning actually becomes a murderer! Who, however, would suspect him of murderous intent? Who could possibly imagine that he had deliberately killed a complete stranger merely to satisfy his lust to kill? Could his action be interpreted in any way other than that of a kindly man bent only on keeping a fellow human being from being run over? There is no ground to suppose even that he would be reproached by the dead! Rather, I should imagine that the old woman would have died with a word of thanks on her lips . . . despite her having been murdered.

Gentlemen, do you now see the beauty of my line of reasoning? Most people seem to believe that whenever a man commits a crime he is sure to be apprehended and swiftly punished. Few, very few, seem to realize that many murderers could go scot-free, if only they would adopt the right tactics. Can you deny this? As can be imagined from the two instances which I have just cited, there are almost limitless ways of committing perfect crimes. For myself, as soon as I discovered the secret I was overjoyed. How generous the Creator was, I told myself blasphemously, to have provided so much opportunity for the perpetration of crimes which can never be detected. Yes, I was quite mad with joy at this discovery. "How wonderful!" I kept repeating. And I knew that once I had put my theories into practice the lives of most people would be completely at the mercy of my whims! Gradually it dawned on me that *murder* offered a key to the problem of relieving my perpetual boredom. Not any ordinary type of murder, I told myself, but murder which would baffle even Sherlock himself! A perfect cure for drowsiness!

During the three years that followed, I gave myself up completely to intensive research in the science of homicide—a pursuit which promptly made me forget my previous boredom. Visualizing myself in the role of a modern Borgia, I swore that I would slay a hundred people before I was done. The only difference, however, would be that instead of using poison, I would kill with the weapon of criminal strategy.

Soon I began my career of crime, and just three months ago I marked up a score of ninety-nine lives snuffed out without anyone's knowing that I had been responsible for these deaths. To make the toll an even hundred I had just one more murder to commit. But putting this question aside for a moment, would you like to hear how I killed the first ninety-nine? Of course, I had no grudge against any of them. My only interest was in the art of killing and nothing else. Consequently, I did not adopt the same method twice! Each time my technique differed, for the very effort of thinking up new ways of killing filled my heart with an unholy pleasure.

Actually, however, I cannot take the time to explain each of the ninety-nine ways of murder I used one after another. Therefore I will merely cite four or five of the most outstanding techniques of murder I devised.

A blind masseur who happened to live in my neighborhood became my first victim. As is frequently the case with persons who are incapacitated, he was a very stubborn fellow. For example, if out of kindness someone cautioned him against a certain act, it was his established rule to do exactly the opposite in a manner which plainly said: "Don't make fun of me because I am blind. I can get along without any advice."

One day, while strolling down a busy thoroughfare, I happened to notice the stubborn masseur coming from the opposite direction. Like the conceited fool he was, he was walking fairly swiftly down the road, with his stick on his shoulder, and was humming a song. Not far ahead of him I saw that a deep pit had been dug on the right-hand side of the street by a gang of workers who were repairing the city's sewers. As he was blind and could not see the sign "Danger! Under Repair!" he kept going straight toward the pit, completely free from care. Suddenly a bright idea struck me.

"Hello, Mr. Nemoto," I called in a familiar tone, for I had often had him massage me. The next moment, before he could even return my greeting, I gave my warning. "Look out!" I shouted. "Step aside to the left! Step aside to the left!" This, of course, I called out in a tone of voice which sounded as if I were joking.

Just as I had suspected, the masseur swallowed the bait. Instead of stepping to the left, he kept on walking without altering his course.

"Ha! ha! ha!" he laughed loudly. "You can't fool me!"

Boldly, he took three extra large steps to the right, purposely ignoring my warning, and the next thing he knew, he had stepped right into the pit dug by the sewer workers.

As soon as he fell in I ran up to the edge of the pit, pretending to be very much alarmed and concerned. In my heart, however, I wondered if I had succeeded in killing him. Deep down at the bottom of the hole I saw the man lying crumpled up in a heap, his head bleeding profusely. Looking closer I saw that his nose and mouth were also covered with blood, and his face was a livid, unhealthy yellow. Poor devil! In his fall, he had bitten off his tongue!

A crowd soon gathered, and after much effort we managed to haul him up to the street. When we stretched him out on the pavement he was still breathing, but very faintly. Someone ran off to call an ambulance, but it arrived too late: the poor masseur was no longer of this world.

Thus my plan had worked successfully. And who was there to suspect me? Had I not always been on the best of terms with the man, using his services often? Also, wasn't it I who had directed him to step aside to the left in an effort to save him from falling into the pit? With such a perfect setup, even the shrewdest detective could not have suspected even for a fleeting moment that behind my words of "kindly warning" there had lurked a coldly calculated intention to kill!

Oh, what a terrible way to amuse oneself! And yet, how merry it was! The joy I felt whenever I conceived a new strategy for murder was akin to that of an artist inspired with a new idea for a painting. As for the nervous strain I underwent on each separate occasion, it was doubly compensated for by the overwhelming satisfaction I derived from my successes. Another horrible aspect of my criminal career was that I would invariably look back on the death scenes I had created and, like a vampire smacking his lips after a feast, relish the memory of how the innocent victims of my ruthlessness had spilled their precious life-blood.

Now I shall switch to a new chapter. The season was summer. Accompanied by an old friend of mine, whom I had already selected as my next victim, I went to a remote fishing village in the province of Awa for a vacation. On the beach we found few visitors from the city; most of the swimmers were well-tanned youngsters from the village. Occasionally, along the coast, we saw a few stray students, sketch-books in hand, engrossed in the scenery.

From every viewpoint it was a very lonely, dull place. One big drawback was that there were hardly any of the attractive girls one finds at the more noted bathing resorts. As for our inn, it was like the cheapest of Tokyo boardinghouses; the food was unsavory, and nothing, with the sole exception of the fresh raw fish they served, seemed to suit our taste. My friend, however, seemed to be enjoying his stay, never suspecting that I had purposely enticed him here for but one purpose—to murder him.

One day I took him out to a place where the shore suddenly ended in cliffs, quite a distance from the village. Quickly I took off my clothes, shouting: "This is an ideal place for diving!" and stood poised to leap into the water below.

"You're right!" my friend replied. "This is indeed a wonderful place for diving!" And he too began stripping off his clothes.

After standing on the edge of the precipice for a moment, I stretched my arms above my head and shouted in my loudest voice: "One, two, three!" And the next moment I dove head-first into the water, managing a fairly graceful swan dive. As soon as my head touched the water, however, I twisted my body into an upward curve, so that I actually allowed myself to submerge to a depth of only about four feet. I swam a little at this depth before rising. For me this shallow dive was no marvelous feat, for I had mastered the technique in my early highschool days. When I finally popped my head out of the water at a distance of about thirty feet from the shore, I wiped the water off my face and, treading water with my feet, called to my friend.

"Come on in," I shouted. "You can dive as deep as you like. This place is almost bottomless!"

Not suspecting anything, my friend quickly nodded and, poising on the edge of the cliff, dove in. He shot into the water with a splash, but did not reappear for a considerable length of time. This, of course, was no surprise to me, for I knew that there was a large, jagged rock located at a depth of only about eight feet, but quite impossible to detect from atop the cliff. I had probed this sector of the water previously, and everything had suited my plans.

As you may know, the better the diver, the shallower he dives into the water. Being an expert, I had managed to surface without coming into contact with the dangerous rock. But my friend, who was only a novice, had dived into the water to the fullest depth. The result was only natural—death from a crushed skull.

Sure enough, after I had waited for some time, he rose to the surface like a dead tunny, drifting at the mercy of the waves. Playing the role of would-be rescuer, I grabbed him and dragged his floating corpse to the shore. Then, leaving him on the sand, I ran back to the village and sounded the alarm. Promptly some fishermen who happened to be resting after a busy morning of hauling in their nets answered my call for help and accompanied me back to the beach. All along, however, I knew that my friend was beyond all earthly help. Crumpled up on the shore just as I had left him, his head crushed like an eggshell, he was indeed a pitiful sight. Taking just one look, the fishermen all shook their heads.

"There's nothing we can do," they said. "He's already dead!"

In all my life I have been questioned by the police only twice, and this was one of those occasions. As I was the sole witness of the "accident," it was only natural that they should question me. But since the victim and I were known to have been great friends, I was quickly exonerated.

"It is quite obvious," the unsuspecting police said, "that you city folks could not have been aware of the presence of that rock," and the coroner's verdict was "accidental death."

Ironically, I was even offered the condolences of the police officers who had cleared me of all possible guilt. "We're very sorry you have lost your friend" were their very words.

Inwardly, I shrieked with laughter.

Well, as I have said, if I were to recite all my murders one after another, I'm afraid there would be no end. By this time you must surely know what I meant when I spoke of perfect crimes. Every murder that I committed was ingeniously planned beforehand so as to leave no trace of evidence. Once, when I was among the spectators of a circus, I captured the attention of a female tight-rope walker who was balancing herself on a high wire by suddenly adopting an extraordinarily queer posture—a posture so queer and obscene that I am ashamed to describe it here. The result, of course, was that she slipped and crashed to her death, because it had been her special pride to walk a tight-rope without the benefit of a net. On another occasion, at the scene of a fire, I calmly informed a shrieking woman searching for her child that I had seen him sleeping inside the house. Believing me instantly, she rushed into the flames, while I egged her on with "Can't you hear him crying? He's wailing and wailing for you!" The woman, of course, was burnt to death. And the ironical part of it all was that her child had been safe and sound all along elsewhere.

Another example I could give is the time I saw a girl on the point of trying to decide whether or not to commit suicide by leaping into a river. At the crucial moment, when she had nearly decided to abandon her attempt, I shouted: "Wait!" Caught by surprise, the girl became flustered and, without any further hesitation, dived into the water and was drowned. This, again, was another demonstration of how one seemingly innocent word can end a person's life.

Well, as you may have realized by this time, there is practically no end to my stories. For another thing, the clock on the wall reminds me that the time is getting late. So I'll conclude my narration for this evening with just one more example of how I killed without arousing any suspicion—only this time it is mass murder of which I'll speak.

This case took place last spring. Perhaps you may even remember the report in the newspapers at that time of how a train on the Tokyo-Karuizawa line jumped the tracks and overturned, taking a heavy toll of lives. Well, that's the catastrophe to which I refer.

Actually, this was the simplest trick of all, although it took me a considerable length of time to select a suitable location to carry out my plot. From the very start, however, I had believed I would find it along the line to Karuizawa; this railway ran through lonely mountains, an ideal condition for my plan, and besides, the line had quite a reputation for frequent accidents.

Finally I decided on a precipice near Kumano-Taira Station. As there was a decent spa near the station, I put up at an inn there and pretended to be a long-staying visitor, bathing in the mineral waters daily. After biding my time for about ten days, I felt it would be safe to begin. So one day I took a walk along a mountain path in the area.

After about an hour's walk I arrived at the top of a high cliff a few miles from the inn. Here I waited until the evening shadows fell. Just beneath the cliff the railway tracks formed a sharp curve. On the other side of the tracks yawned a deep ravine, with a swiftly-flowing stream in the mist beyond.

After a while the zero hour I had decided on arrived. Although there was no one there to see, I pretended to stumble and kicked a large rock which had been lying in such a position that this was enough to roll it off the cliff, right down onto the railway tracks. I had planned to repeat the operation over and over again with other rocks if necessary, but I quickly perceived with a thrill that the rock had fallen onto one of the rails, just where I had wanted it.

A down train was scheduled to come along those tracks in half an hour. In the dark, and with the rock lying on the other side of the curve, it would be impossible for the engineer to notice it. After I had thus set the stage for my crime I hurried to Kumano-Taira Station—I knew the walk would take me over half an hour— dashed into the stationmaster's office, and blurted out: "Something terrible has happened!"

All the railway officials looked up anxiously and asked me what I meant.

"I'm a visitor at the spa here," I said, breathing heavily. "I was taking a walk a short while ago along the edge of the cliff above the railway line about four miles from here. Accidentally I stumbled and kicked a rock off the cliff down onto the tracks. Almost immediately I realized that if a train passed there, it would be derailed. So I tried desperately to find a path down to the spot so as to remove the rock, but as I am a stranger in these parts, I could find no way down. Knowing there was not a moment to be lost, I came here as fast as my legs could carry me to warn you. Surely you people can do something to avert a catastrophe."

When I had finished talking the stationmaster paled. "This is a serious matter," he gasped. "The down train just passed this station.

By this time it must already have reached that spot!" This, of course, was exactly what I had expected to hear.

Suddenly the phone rang, but even before anyone picked up the receiver, I knew what the report would be. Yes, the worst had happened! The train had jumped the tracks, and two of the coaches had overturned.

Soon I was taken to the village police station for questioning. But my deed had been perpetrated only after long and careful deliberation, so I had all the answers ready. After the interrogation I was released. I had, of course, been severely admonished, but that was all.

So, with just one rock, I had succeeded in taking the lives of no less than seventeen persons in just that one "accident."

Gentlemen, the grand total of the murders I have so far committed numbers ninety-nine. Rather than being penitent, however, I have only become bored with my festival of blood. Today I have but one desire, to make the score an even hundred . . . by taking my own life.

Yes, you may well knit your brows, after hearing of all my cruel acts. Surely not even the devil himself could have surpassed me in villainy. And yet, I still insist that all my wickedness was but the result of unbearable boredom. I killed—but only for the sake of killing! I harbored no malice toward any of my victims. In short, murder was, for me, a sort of game. Do you think I am mad? A homicidal maniac? Of course you do. But I do not care, for I believe I am in good company. Birds of a feather, you know . . .

On this cynical and insulting note the narrator concluded his disgusting story, his narrow, bloodshot eyes gazing suspiciously into ours.

Suddenly, on the surface of the silk curtains near the door, something began to glitter. At first it looked like a large, silver coin, then like a full moon peering out of the red curtains. Gradually I recognized the mysterious object as a large silver tray held in both hands by a waitress, magically come, as if from nowhere, to serve us drinks. For a fleeting moment I visualized a scene from *Salome*, with the dancing girl carrying the freshly severed head of the prophet on a tray. I even thought that after the tray there would appear from out of the silk curtains a glittering Damascene broadsword, or at least an old Chinese halberd. Gradually my eyes became more accustomed to the wraith-like figure of the waitress, and I gasped with admiration, for she was indeed a beauty! Without any explanation, she moved gracefully among the seven of us and began to serve drinks.

As I took a glass I noticed that my hand was trembling. What strange magic was this, I pondered. Who was she? And where did she come from? Was she from some imaginary world, or was she one of the hostesses from the restaurant downstairs?

Suddenly Tanaka spoke in a casual tone, not at all different from the voice he had used to tell his story—but the words he uttered startled me.

"Now I will shoot you!" were the very words he spoke, having first drawn a revolver from his pocket and aimed it at the girl.

The next instance our cries of surprise, the explosion of the revolver, and the piercing shriek of the girl all seemed to merge. All of us leapt from our seats and lunged at the madman. But then we stopped in our tracks. There, before our eyes, was the woman who had been shot, alive and well, but with a blank look on her face.

"Ha! ha! ha!" Tanaka suddenly burst out laughing in the hysterical tone of a madman. "It's only a toy, only a toy. Ha! ha! You were taken in nicely, Hanako. Ha! ha! . . ."

Was the revolver, then, only a toy, I wondered. From all appearances, it had certainly looked real—with the smoke curling out of the muzzle.

"What a start you gave me!" the waitress cried. She then tried to laugh, but her voice sounded hollow. As for her face, it was as white as a rice cake.

After a moment she went up to Tanaka hesitantly and asked to examine the weapon. Tanaka complied, and the girl looked at the pistol closely.

"Oh, it certainly looks like the real thing, doesn't it?" she exclaimed. "I had no idea it was only a toy." In a playful gesture she suddenly pointed the six-chambered revolver at Tanaka and said: "Now, I'll shoot you and return the compliment."

Bending her left arm, she rested the barrel of the revolver on her elbow and aimed at Tanaka's chest, smiling mischievously.

Instead of showing fright, Tanaka only smiled. "Go on, shoot me!" he said teasingly.

"Why not?" the girl retorted, laughing.

Bang! Again the loud explosion seemed to split our eardrums.

This time Tanaka rose from his chair, staggered a couple of steps, and then fell to the floor with a thud. At first we only laughed, although we felt that the joke was becoming stale. But Tanaka continued to remain stretched out on the floor, perfectly still and lifeless, and we again began to feel restless. Was it another of his tricks? It was hard to tell, for it was all uncomfortably realistic. In spite of ourselves, we soon knelt down beside him although we did not exactly know what to do.

The man who had been sitting next to me took the candelabrum from the table and held it up. By its light we found Tanaka sprawled out grotesquely on the floor, his face contorted. The next moment we got the worst fright of all when we saw his blood oozing out of his chest, dripping onto the floor to form a pool.

From all these indications, we quickly surmised that in the second chamber of the revolver, which he had passed off as only a toy, there had been a real bullet. For a long while we stood there, dumbfounded.

Gradually, I began to reason. Had this all been part of Tanaka's program for the night from the very start? Had he actually been carrying out his threat of ultimately taking his own life to make his score of killings an even hundred? But why did he choose this Red Chamber as the scene for his final deed? Had it been his intention to pin the crime on the waitress? But certainly she was innocent, for she had not known the pistol was real when she shot him.

Suddenly, I began to see the light. Tanaka's favorite bag of tricks! Yes, that's what it was! Similar to all his other crimes, he had used the waitress to murder him, and yet had made sure that she would not be punished. With six of us as witnesses, she would, of course, be exonerated. Reasoning thus, I knew that I could not be wrong. The "super-killer" had killed for the last time. Each of the other men also seemed to be wrapped in deep meditation. Plainly, I could read their thoughts as being the same as mine.

An eerie silence fell over the company. On the floor the waitress, who had unwittingly become a murderess, was weeping hysterically beside the body of her victim. In all aspects, the tragedy which had occurred in the candle-lit Red Chamber seemed altogether too fantastic to be a happening of this world.

All of a sudden a strange voice drowned out the waitress's loud sobs. With an icy chill creeping down my back, I stole a glance at Tanaka, and this time I nearly fainted. Slowly, the "dead man" was staggering to his feet. . . .

In the next tense moment, the "corpse" broke the suspense by bursting into laughter, holding his sides as if to prevent himself from splitting. He then turned to us and said mockingly: "You are indeed a naive audience!"

No sooner had he spoken than another surprise was in store for us. This time the waitress, who had been sobbing on the floor, also got to her feet and began to shake with convulsions of laughter. Rubbing our eyes, we automatically, like robots, returned our gaze to Tanaka.

"What—what happened?" I asked sheepishly. "Are we all bewitched?"

In answer Tanaka said: "Look at this." Still chuckling, he held out a nondescript reddish mass on the palm of his hand and invited us to examine it. "It's a small bag made of the bladder of a cow," he explained. "A few moments ago it contained tomato ketchup and was planted inside my shirt. When the girl fired the blank cartridge, I pressed the bag and pretended to be bleeding. . . . And now, one more confession. The complete life story which I related this evening was nothing but a mass of fabrications from beginning to end. But you must admit I was a pretty good actor. You see, gentlemen, as I had been informed that you were all suffering from boredom, I merely tried to give you some excitement. . . ."

After Tanaka had explained all his tricks, the waitress who had served as his accomplice suddenly pressed the wall-switch. Without warning, a blaze of lights caught all of us huddled in the center of the fantastic room, blinking foolishly at each other. For the first time since joining the group I realized how artificial everything looked in our so-called room of mystery. And as for ourselves, we were just a bunch of fools. . . .

Shortly after Tanaka and the waitress bade us good night, we held a special meeting. This time, no stories were told. Instead, we unanimously agreed to disband.

*Naoya Shiga* (1883–1971), *one of Japan's great short story writers, has had a major influence on modern Japanese literature. He wrote in a spare, intense, highly personal style, often producing stories that are part fiction and part essay. "The Razor" and "Han's Crime," published early in his career, are atypical of his work in that they are not autobiographical. In these two stories, Shiga attempts to probe the depths of human nature and asks if an individual can be considered guilty of a crime if he acts out of deep-seated or unconscious motivation.*

*Shiga's only full-length novel is* A Dark Night's Passing *(1922–1937). Written over a period of many years, it tells the story of the long estrangement between him and his father, and has been hailed as a masterpiece by several critics. The novel was translated into English in 1976, and translations of ten of his best short stories can be found in William F. Sibley's* The Shiga Hero *(1979).*

# The Razor

## by NAOYA SHIGA

### TRANSLATED BY WILLIAM F. SIBLEY

Yoshisaburo of the Tatsu Barbershop in Roppongi had taken to his bed with a cold. Of all times to be sick, and he hardly ever was, it was the eve of the ceremonies for the imperial ancestors, the peak season for the military trade. On his sickbed he now regretted having dismissed, only recently, his two assistants, Gen and Jita.

Yoshisaburo was only slightly older than they, and had himself been apprenticed at the Tatsu until the former master, much impressed with his skillful wielding of the razor, had given him his only daughter's hand in marriage and, at the same time, passed on the management of the shop. The assistant Gen, who had quietly had his eyes on the daughter himself, resigned not long after. Jita, a

51

much more mild-mannered fellow, had soon learned to call his former colleague "boss," and stayed on. Within half a year the former proprietor died, and his wife but a few months later.

Yoshisaburo truly was a master with the razor. And fastidious to a fault. Should a customer's face be ever so slightly rough to the touch after a shave, he would finish by all but plucking out each remaining whisker one by one. He gave such close shaves that the customers would say he had spared them a day's growth; yet they never complained of any irritation to the skin, nor had he in ten years on the job so much as nicked a man's face. His record was spotless.

Two years after Yoshisaburo took over, his onetime fellow apprentice Gen reappeared. In view of their long association, he could only accept the man's apologies and take him back into the shop. In the meantime, however, Gen had changed a good deal, and for the worse. He tended to shirk his duties, and began to entice Jita along on his frequent visits to the ladies of doubtful virtue over at Kasumi-cho, where the soldiers went. When it came to Jita's taking money from the shop for these escapades, at Gen's instigation, Yoshisaburo spoke up and repeatedly warned the more gentle and impressionable of his assistants. But it was too late. Jita had acquired the habit of putting his hand in the till and, a month or so ago, had been dismissed along with Gen.

Yoshisaburo was now making do with a very pale young man of about twenty, named Kanejiro, who was singularly lacking in energy, and a thirteen-year-old boy named Kin, whose abnormally elongated head likewise failed to inspire confidence. As he lay tossing feverishly on his bed, he worried to himself that now, at this busy season before the holiday, the likes of these two could scarcely be expected to fill in for him.

Toward noon, customers crowded into the shop. The rattle of the glass door opening and closing and the scuffing of Kin's worn clogs as he shuffled to and fro grated on Yoshisaburo's frayed nerves. Again the shop door opened, and a woman was heard announcing herself as a servant from the Yamada household in Ryudomachi. "The master is off on a journey tomorrow evening," she said. "Please sharpen this by tonight. I'll come back for it." To

Kanejiro's reply that they were very busy and would do it by next morning, if that were agreeable, she reluctantly assented: "Very well, if you're quite sure."

No sooner had she closed the door behind her than she opened it again and called in to Kanejiro, "I don't like to bother him, but could you ask the boss to do it?"

"I'm afraid that the boss . . ."

"Kane! I'll do it," Yoshisaburo shouted from his bed in a hard, hoarse voice.

"Yes ma'am! We'll see to it," said the assistant. Again the door closed behind her.

Yoshisaburo cursed softly to himself. He stretched out his pale, grimy forearm against the silk lining of the coverlet and contemplated it awhile. He was aware of his fever-leeched body as of a dead weight apart from himself. His eyes focused intently on the soot-stained paper dog hanging from the ceiling. It was encrusted with flies.

He half-listened to the conversation going on in the shop out front. A few soldiers were weighing the various merits of local restaurants and bemoaning the rotten army rations—though since the weather had grown chilly, one of them allowed, you could just manage to get the stuff down. Somewhat soothed by this talk, Yoshisaburo lazily rolled over.

He savored his new tranquillity and watched his wife, Oume, bathed in the milky twilight that filtered through the doorway of the adjoining small kitchen, as she went about preparing dinner, the baby still strapped to her back. "I'd better get it over with," he said to himself. But the effort of raising his leaden body to a sitting position made him dizzy, and he flopped back against the pillow.

Oume came in from the kitchen, dangling her wet hands before her, and gently asked if he needed help to the toilet. Yoshisaburo tried to say no, but he could barely hear his own voice. When his wife had removed the covers and pushed aside the basin and the medicine bottles by his bed, he said again, "No, it's not that." But again his hoarse voice seemed not to reach her. His brief spell of tranquillity was shattered.

"Let me pull you up from behind," Oume said in a cajoling

tone. With what little force he could muster, Yoshisaburo hurled back at her, "Bring me the leather strap and Mr. Yamada's razor. Now."

After a moment's silence, Oume ventured, "But are you up to it?"

"Never mind! Bring them *now.*"

"Well, if you're going to get up you'll really have to put on a bed jacket . . ."

"Didn't you hear what I told you!" This in a hushed voice taut with anger and frustration.

Undaunted, Oume wrapped the bed jacket over his shoulders from behind as he sat up and prepared himself for the chore. Yoshisaburo stiffly hoisted one hand to the collar of the jacket and tossed the garment off.

Without a word, Oume slid open the dividing partition and went down into the shop, returned with the leather strap, and, as there was clearly nowhere to hang it, set about nailing a small hook into the wooden supporting post next to the bed.

Even when he was well, Yoshisaburo found this particular task irksome if he was not in the right mood; now, with his hands trembling feverishly, he made no progress at all. Painfully aware of his mounting irritation, Oume repeatedly urged him to leave the task to the assistant Kane. Her husband made no reply. But after fifteen minutes or so his strength gave out. With a look of utter exhaustion, he sank back onto his bed and dozed off.

Yamada's maid, on the pretext that she happened to be passing by, came to fetch the razor early in the evening.

Oume boiled some rice gruel for her sick husband but could not bring herself to wake him from his much needed sleep—and, almost certainly, risk incurring his wrath again. And so she put the meal aside and left him alone, until about eight o'clock, when she began to worry about the medicine he was supposed to take. Woken from a sound sleep by his wife's persistent shaking, Yoshisaburo was unexpectedly docile. As soon as he had eaten he lay down and went back to sleep.

A little before ten he was roused again and given more medicine. Idle thoughts drifted through his mind. There was an unpleasant sensation of his own warm breath trapped around his face by the coverlet, which he had pulled up to just below his eyes. He cast a listless gaze around him. The black leather strap was still there, hanging from the post, solid, motionless. The lamp gave off a murky, cloying orange light that shone on his wife's back as she sat in a corner nursing the baby. The whole room seemed smothered in fever.

From the narrow earthen passageway between the house and the shop the apprentice Kin called out in a quavering voice. Yoshisaburo's response, hoarse and muffled by the coverlet, could not be heard at first and had to be repeated.

"What is it!" he managed at length to say in a sharp, distinct tone.

"Mr. Yamada's razor is back again."

"Another one?"

"No, the same. He said he tried it right away and it wouldn't shave very well. He doesn't need it till tomorrow noon, so he'd like you to have another look at it."

Having ascertained that the Yamada maid had already gone home, he said, "All right, let's have a look." He stretched his arms out over the covers to take the razor case from the boy, who was crouched down on hands and knees at the foot of the bed.

"But your hands aren't steady," said Oume, doing up her robe as she came over to his side. "Wouldn't it be better to ask Mr. Yoshikawa at Kasumi-cho to do it?"

Yoshiaburo ignored her and reached out to turn up the wick of the gas lamp. He took the razor from the case and turned it this way and that under the light. Oume sat down by his pillow and placed a hand on his forehead. With his free hand he brushed hers away in a show of annoyance. He ordered Kin, still in attendance at the foot of the bed, to bring him a whetstone at once.

When the whetstone had been set out, Yoshisaburo got up; resting one knee on the tatami, he began to sharpen the razor. The clock struck ten in slow even measure. Oume sat looking on in silence. She knew it was pointless to say anything more.

After applying the razor to the whetstone awhile, he went back to the leather strap. The slapping sound of the razor against the strap seemed to revive the stagnant atmosphere of the room. In vain Yoshisaburo strained to steady his trembling hand, to adjust himself to the rhythm of the task. Then, suddenly, the hook that Oume had attached to the post came loose; the strap flew off and wrapped itself around the razor.

"Look out!" cried Oume. Afterward she glanced fearfully at her husband. His brow contracted into a scowl full of tension.

Yoshisaburo extricated the razor from the strap and, wearing only the thin bed jacket, started toward the shop.

"But you *mustn't*," Oume half-sobbed.

Yoshiaburo paid no attention. He went down across the narrow passage into the shop, Oume following behind him. Not a single customer remained. The apprentice Kin sat lackadaisically in one of the barber chairs, facing the mirror.

When Oume asked where Kane was, young Kin replied, almost solemnly, "He's gone courting Tokiko."

"He told you that himself?"

Oume chuckled. Her husband maintained his tense expression.

"Tokiko" was a woman of uncertain background—said to have once been a proper little schoolgirl—whose ménage now ran, a few doors away, what purported to be a military provisions shop. She invariably had a couple of young men sitting around in the shop: soldiers, students, working men from the neighborhood.

"Well, go tell him to come back and close up," Oume directed.

"No. It's too early."

At this automatic negative response from her husband, Oume fell silent.

Yoshisaburo resumed his sharpening, which went somewhat better now that he was seated in the shop. His wife produced a padded cotton jacket and contrived at some length, as with an unruly child, to slip his arms into the sleeves. With a look of relief she sat down on the raised threshold, from where she could keep a watchful eye on the sick man's face as he threw himself into his task.

Curled up on the customer's bench next to the window, Kin exposed one leg, on which he practiced shaving, drawing his razor slowly up and down over the smooth, hairless skin.

Presently the shop door rattled briskly open and in walked a short, stocky workingman who looked to be in his early twenties. Wearing a thickly woven unpadded robe tied with an ordinary sash of cheap fabric, he balanced his feet precariously on clogs whose thongs were shrunken beyond repair.

"S'pose you could take a minute or two for a once-over-lightly?" The man stood in front of the mirror thrusting his chin out and rubbing it insistently with his fingertips. Below the facade of city mannerisms his accent revealed he was nothing but a peasant; his bony knuckles and coarse, dark complexion spoke of heavy day labor.

"Best fetch Kane right away." Oume entreated as much with her eyes as her words.

"I'll do it myself."

"Now please, you're not yourself today."

"I said I'll do it."

Cut off sharply. Oume muttered to herself. When Yoshisaburo ordered her to bring his white jacket, she temporized, "But he said he only wanted a quick shave—you won't need it for that," She hoped at least to keep him in the quilted garment.

The young man watched this exchange with an odd, quizzical expression; blinking his small, sunken eyes in a display of solicitude, he asked if the chief barber were sick.

"Oh, just a touch of a cold," said Yoshisaburo.

"They say there's a mean one going around, that's what they say, so you'd better take care of yourself!"

"I appreciate your concern," Yoshisaburo answered in a chilly tone.

As he was putting on his white jacket, the young man gave him a suggestive smirk and reiterated that he was in a great hurry; a quick going over would do.

Yoshisaburo said nothing and put the finishing touches on the blade, rubbing it against the flat of his arm.

"Let's see," the young man maundered on, "if I get out by ten-thirty I can still make it by eleven-thirty . . ."

Yoshisaburo would have liked to tell his customer a thing or two.

The figure of an ugly woman inside a small hovel of a

whorehouse flashed before his mind's eye. She spoke in an unpleasantly androgynous voice. In his fever-wracked imagination the presentiment that she would shortly be joined by this vulgar little wretch conjured up a sequence of revolting scenes. He plunged a cake of soap into water that was by now stone cold, and proceeded with abandon to smear lather over the man's face from under the chin up to the cheeks. Even now the fellow was straining to peek at his face in the mirror. Yoshisaburo could hardly keep from spewing out his disgust.

With a few more slaps of the razor against the strap, he began to shave the man's throat. The blade did not cut well. His hand trembled. And, as he bent over the chair, mucus began to drip from his nostrils, as it had not when he was lying down. He paused now and then to wipe it away, but as soon as he picked up the razor again he could feel new drops forming at the nostrils.

At the sound of the baby crying, Oume went back into the house. Yoshisaburo was overcome by a fresh wave of loathing. The man showed not the slightest awareness that he was being shaved with a dull blade, no sign of pain or irritation appeared on his face. As though his nerve endings were dead. There were other, sharper razors Yoshisaburo could use. But why bother; what did it matter? And so he went on with this blunt instrument. But he began to wield it with some caution, almost in spite of himself. For he sensed that the smallest nick on the man's face would rankle within himself, and would end by inciting him to still further hatred. He felt new fatigue in body and spirit, and his fever seemed to have returned.

After several vain attempts at conversation, the young man had at last been chastened by the barber's unfriendly demeanor and ceased his chatter. By the time the shaving reached the upper part of his face, he had succumbed to his exhaustion from the heavy work of the day and drifted off. Kin had meanwhile stretched out by the window and fallen asleep. Back inside the house the murmurings of Oume comforting the baby had died away. The stillness of the night spread through the shop and house and all around outside. Only the scraping of the razor was to be heard.

As this new fatigue enveloped him, Yoshisaburo's anger and

irritation gave way to a feeling of being on the verge of tears. His eyes misted over and seemed about to melt away from the inside with fever.

Having shaved most of the throat, the chin, cheeks and brow, he contemplated the patch of soft flesh on the throat which he had left to the end. It was a very stubborn spot. Possessed by his task and its loathsome object, he had an impulse to slice the little patch off, skin and all, an impulse powerfully reinforced by a glance at the face below him, full of coarse pores brimming wth oil. By this point the young man had fallen into a deep sleep. His head lolled back against the chair and his mouth was agape, giving him an air of childlike vulnerability. His teeth were stained and crooked.

Yoshisaburo was bone tired and at his wits' end. He felt as if poison had been injected into all his joints. He could have thrown everything aside that very second and sunk to the floor. Enough! On the point of calling a halt any number of times, he persisted out of a combination of inertia and obsession.

A soft nicking sound and a sensation of the razor catching against the skin. The young man's throat twitched. A mercurial shudder surged through Yoshisaburo's body from head to toe. At that moment all his physical fatigue, and his paralysis of will as well, were swept away.

The cut was barely half an inch long. Yoshisaburo stood motionless and examined it. The tiny slit in the skin at first turned a milky white; then a little splurt of pale crimson and the blood began to ooze up. He continued to scrutinize. The color of the blood deepened and a distinct drop formed at the slit. The drop swelled until it burst, and the blood streamed down in a single thin strand. At this sight he was shaken by a violent emotion.

The force of this inner onslaught was doubled by his never having experienced such a sight. His breathing quickened. His whole being came to focus on the bleeding cut. He could hold out no longer.

He changed his grip so that the tip pointed downward and in one swift thrust plunged the razor into the young man's throat. It penetrated the length of the blade up to the handle. The man did not move a muscle.

Presently the blood came gushing out from the deep wound. The man's face rapidly turned an ashen hue.

Yoshisaburo sank into the adjacent chair as though in a faint. All the tension drained out of him. At the same time, the fatigue he had felt before returned with a vengeance. With his eyes tightly shut, his body limp and motionless, he too looked dead. Even the night grew still as death. Nothing moved. The world had fallen into a deep slumber. Only the mirrors looking down from three sides of the room reflected this scene in their cold, impassive gaze.

# Han's Crime

## by NAOYA SHIGA

### TRANSLATED BY IVAN MORRIS

Much to everyone's astonishment, the young Chinese juggler, Han, severed his wife's carotid artery with one of his heavy knives in the course of a performance. The young woman died on the spot. Han was immediately arrested.

At the scene of the event were the director of the theatre, Han's Chinese assistant, the announcer and more than three hundred spectators. There was also a policeman who had been stationed behind the audience. Despite the presence of all these witnesses, it was a complete mystery whether the killing had been intentional or accidental.

Han's act was as follows: his wife would stand in front of a wooden board about the size of a door and, from a distance of approximately four yards, he would throw his large knives at her so that they stuck in the board about two inches apart, forming a contour around her body. As each knife left his hand, he would let out a staccato exclamation as if to punctuate his performance.

The examining judge first questioned the director of the theatre.

"Would you say that this was a very difficult act?"

"No, Your Honour, it's not as difficult as all that for an experienced performer. But to do it properly, you want steady nerves and complete concentration."

"I see. Then assuming that what happened was an accident, it was an extremely unlikely type of accident?"

"Yes, indeed, Your Honour. If accidents were not so very unlikely, I should never have allowed the act in my theatre."

"Well then, do you consider that this was done on purpose?"

"No, Your Honour, I do not. And for this reason: an act of this kind performed at a distance of twelve feet requires not only skill but at the same time a certain—well, intuitive sense. It is true that we all thought a mistake virtually out of the question, but after what has happened, I think we must admit that there was always the possibility of a mistake."

"Well then, which do you think it was—a mistake or on purpose?"

"That I simply cannot say, Your Honour."

The judge felt puzzled. Here was a clear case of homicide, but whether it was manslaughter or premeditated murder it was impossible to tell. If murder, it was indeed a clever one, thought the judge.

Next, the judge decided to question the Chinese assistant who had worked with Han for many years past.

"What was Han's normal behaviour?" he asked.

"He was always very correct, Your Honour; he didn't gamble or drink or run after women. Besides, last year he took up Christianity. He studied English and in his free time always seemed to be reading collections of sermons—the Bible and that sort of thing."

"And what about his wife's behaviour?"

"Also very correct, Your Honour. Strolling players aren't always the most moral people, as you know. Mrs. Han was a pretty little woman and quite a few men used to make propositions to her, but she never paid the slightest attention to that kind of thing."

"And what sort of temperaments did they have?"

"Always very kind and gentle, Sir. They were extremely good to all their friends and acquaintances and never quarrelled with anyone. But . . ." He broke off and reflected a moment before continuing. "Your Honour, I'm afraid that if I tell you this, it may go badly for Han. But to be quite truthful, these two people, who were so gentle and unselfish to others, were amazingly cruel in their relations to each other."

"Why was that?"

"I don't know, Your Honour."

"Was that the case ever since you first knew them?"

"No, Your Honour. About two years ago Mrs. Han was pregnant. The child was born prematurely and died after about three days. That marked a change in their relations. They began having terrible rows over the most trivial things, and Han's face used to turn white as a sheet. He always ended by suddenly growing silent. He never once raised his hand against her or anything like that—I suppose it would have gone against his principles. But when you looked at him, Your Honour, you could see the terrible anger in his eyes! It was quite frightening at times.

"One day I asked Han why he didn't separate from his wife, seeing that things were so bad between them. Well, he told me that he had no real grounds for divorce, even though his love for her had died. Of course, she felt this and gradually stopped loving him too. He told me all this himself. I think the reason he began reading the Bible and all those sermons was to calm the violence in his heart and stop himself from hating his wife, whom he had no real cause to hate. Mrs. Han was really a pathetic woman. She had been with Han nearly three years and had travelled all over the country with him as a strolling player. If she'd ever left Han and gone back home, I don't think she'd have found it easy to get married. How many men would trust a woman who'd spent all that time travelling about? I suppose that's why she stayed with Han, even though they got on so badly."

"And what do you really think about this killing?"

"You mean, Your Honour, do I think it was an accident or done on purpose?"

"That's right."

"Well, Sir, I've been thinking about it from every angle since the day it happened. The more I think, the less I know what to make of it. I've talked about it with the announcer, and he also says he can't understand what happened."

"Very well. But tell me this: at the actual moment it did happen, did it occur to you to wonder whether it was accidental or on purpose?"

"Yes, Sir, it did. I thought, 'He's gone and killed her.'"

"On purpose you mean?"

"Yes, Sir. However, the announcer says that he thought, 'His hands slipped.'"

"Yes, but he didn't know about their everyday relations as you did."

"That may be, Your Honour. But afterwards I wondered if it wasn't just because I did know about those relations that I thought, 'He's killed her.'"

"What were Han's reactions at the moment?"

"He cried out, 'Ha.' As soon as I heard that, I looked up and saw blood gushing from his wife's throat. For a few seconds she kept standing there, then her knees seemed to fold up under her and her body swayed forward. When the knife fell out, she collapsed on the floor, all crumpled in a heap. Of course there was nothing any of us could do—we just sat there petrified, staring at her . . . As to Han, I really can't describe his reactions, for I wasn't looking at him. It was only when the thought struck me, 'He's finally gone and killed her' that I glanced at him. His face was dead white and his eyes closed. The stage manager lowered the curtain. When they picked up Mrs. Han's body she was already dead. Han dropped to his knees then, and for a long time he kept praying in silence."

"Did he appear very upset?"

"Yes, Sir, he was quite upset."

"Very well. If I have anything further to ask you, I shall call for you again."

The judge dismissed the Chinese assistant and now summoned Han himself to the stand. The juggler's intelligent face was drawn and pale; one could tell right away that he was in a state of nervous exhaustion.

"I have already questioned the director of the theatre and your assistant," said the judge when Han had taken his place in the witness-box. "I now propose to examine you."

Han bowed his head.

"Tell me," said the judge, "did you at any time love your wife?"

"From the day of our marriage until the child was born I loved her with all my heart."

"And why did the birth of the child change things?"

"Because I knew it was not mine."

"Did you know who the other man was?"

"I had a very good idea. I think it was my wife's cousin."

"Did you know him personally?"

"He was a close friend. It was he who first suggested that we get married. It was he who urged me to marry her."

"I presume that his relations with her occurred prior to your marriage."

"Yes, Sir. The child was born eight months after we were married."

"According to your assistant, it was a premature birth."

"That is what I told everyone."

"The child died very soon after birth, did it not? What was the cause of death?"

"He was smothered by his mother's breasts."

"Did your wife do that on purpose?"

"She said it was an accident."

The judge was silent and looked fixedly at Han's face. Han raised his head but kept his eyes lowered as he awaited the next question. The judge continued:

"Did your wife confess these relations to you?"

"She did not confess, nor did I ever ask her about them. The child's death seemed like retribution for everything and I decided that I should be as magnanimous as possible, but . . ."

"But in the end you were unable to be magnanimous?"

"That's right. I could not help thinking that the death of the child was insufficient retribution. When apart from my wife, I was able to reason calmly, but as soon as I saw her, something happened inside me. When I saw her body, my temper would begin to rise."

"Didn't divorce occur to you?"

"I often thought that I should like to have a divorce, but I never mentioned it to my wife. My wife used to say that if I left her she could no longer exist."

"Did she love you?"

"She did not love me."

"Then why did she say such things?"

"I think she was referring to the material means of existence. Her home had been ruined by her elder brother and she knew that no serious man would want to marry a woman who had been the wife of a strolling player. Also, her feet were too small for her to do any ordinary work."

"What were your physical relations?"

"I imagine about the same as with most couples."

"Did your wife have any real liking for you?"

"I do not think she really liked me. In fact, I think it must have been very painful for her to live with me as my wife. Still, she endured it. She endured it with a degree of patience almost unthinkable for a man. She used to observe me with a cold, cruel look in her eyes as my life gradually went to pieces. She never showed a flicker of sympathy as she saw me struggling in agony to escape into a better, truer sort of existence."

"Why could you not take some decisive action—have it out with her, or even leave her if necessary?"

"Because my mind was full of all sorts of ideals."

"What ideals?"

"I wanted to behave towards my wife in such a way that there would be no wrong on my side . . . But in the end it didn't work."

"Did you never think of killing your wife?"

Han did not answer and the judge repeated his question. After a long pause, Han replied:

"Before the idea of killing her occurred to me, I often used to think it would be a good thing if she died."

"Well, in that case, if it had not been against the law, don't you think you might have killed her?"

"I wasn't thinking in terms of the law, Sir. That's not what stopped me. It was just that I was weak. At the same time I had this over-mastering desire to enter into a truer sort of life."

"Nevertheless you did think of killing your wife, did you not— later on, I mean?"

"I never made up my mind to do it. But, yes, it is correct to say that I did think about it once."

"How long was that before the event?"

"The previous night . . . Or perhaps even the same morn-ing?"

"Had you been quarrelling?"

"Yes, Sir."

"What about?"

"About something so petty that it's hardly worth mentioning."

"Try telling me about it."

"It was a question of food. I get rather short-tempered when I haven't eaten for some time. Well, that evening my wife had been dawdling and our supper wasn't ready when it should have been. I got very angry."

"Were you more violent than usual?"

"No, but afterwards I still felt worked up, which was unusual. I suppose it was because I'd been worrying so much during those past weeks about making a better existence for myself, and realising there was nothing I could do about it. I went to bed but couldn't get to sleep. All sorts of upsetting thoughts went through my mind. I began to feel that whatever I did, I should never be able to achieve the things I really wanted—that however hard I tried, I should never be able to escape from all the hateful aspects of my present life. This sad, hopeless state of affairs all seemed connected with my marriage. I desperately wanted to find a chink of light to lead me out of my darkness, but even this desire was gradually being extinguished. The hope of escape still flickered and sputtered within me, and I knew that if ever it should go out I would to all intents and purposes be a dead person.

"And then the ugly thought began flitting through my mind, 'If only she would die! If only she would die! If only she would die! Why should I not kill her?' The practical consequences of such a crime meant nothing to me any longer. No doubt I would go to prison, but life in prison could not be worse—could only be better—than this present existence. And yet somehow I had the feeling that killing my wife would solve nothing. It would have been shirking the issue, in the same way as suicide. I must go through each day's suffering as it came, I told myself; there was no way to circumvent that. That had become my true life now: to suffer.

"As my mind raced along these tracks, I almost forgot that the cause of my suffering lay beside me. Utterly exhausted, I lay there unable to sleep. I fell into a blank state of stupefaction, and as my tortured mind turned numb, the idea of killing my wife gradually faded. Then I was overcome by the sad empty feeling that follows a nightmare. I thought of all my fine resolutions for a better life, and realised that I was too weak-hearted to attain it. When dawn finally broke I saw that my wife, also, had not been sleeping . . ."

"When you got up, did you behave normally towards each other?"

"We did not say a single word to each other."

"But why didn't you think of leaving her, when things had come to this?"

"Do you mean, Your Honour, that that would have been a solution of my problem? No, no, that too would have been a shirking of the issue! As I told you, I was determined to behave towards my wife so that there would be no wrong on my side."

Han gazed earnestly at the judge, who nodded his head as a sign for him to continue.

"Next day I was physically exhausted and of course my nerves were ragged. It was agony for me to remain still, and as soon as I had got dressed I left the house and wandered aimlessly about the deserted part of the town. Constantly the thought kept returning that I must do something to solve my life, but the idea of killing no longer occurred to me. The truth is that there was a chasm between my thoughts of murder the night before and any actual decision to commit a crime! Indeed, I never even thought about that evening's performance. If I had, I certainly would have decided to leave out the knife-throwing act. There were dozens of other acts that could have been substituted.

"Well, the evening came and finally it was our turn to appear on the stage. I did not have the slightest premonition that anything out of the ordinary was to happen. As usual, I demonstrated to the audience the sharpness of my knives by slicing pieces of paper and throwing some of the knives at the floor-boards. Presently my wife appeared, heavily made up and wearing an elaborate Chinese costume; after greeting the audience with her charming smile, she took up her position in front of the board. I picked up one of the knives and placed myself at the usual distance from her.

"That's when our eyes met for the first time since the previous evening. At once I understood the risk of having chosen this particular act for that night's performance! Obviously I would have to master my nerves, yet the exhaustion which had penetrated to the very marrow of my bones prevented me. I sensed that I could no longer trust my own arm. To calm myself I closed my eyes for a moment, and I sensed that my whole body was trembling.

"Now the time had come! I aimed my first knife above her head; it struck one inch higher than usual. My wife raised her arms and I prepared to throw my next two knives under each of her arms. As the first one left the ends of my fingers, I felt as if something were holding it back; I no longer had the sense of being able to determine the exact destination of my knives. It was now really a matter of luck if the knife struck at the point intended; each of my movements had become deliberate and self-conscious.

"I threw one knife to the left of my wife's neck and was about to throw another to the right when I saw a strange expression in her eyes. She seemed to be seized by a paroxysm of fear! Did she have a presentiment that this knife, that in a matter of seconds would come hurtling towards her, was going to lodge in her throat? I do not know. All I knew was that her terrible expression of fear was reflected in my own heart. I felt dizzy as if about to faint. Forcing the knife deliberately out of my hand, I as good as aimed it into space . . ."

The judge was silent, peering intently at Han.

"All at once the thought came to me, 'I've killed her,' " said Han abruptly.

"On purpose, you mean?"

"Yes. Suddenly I felt that I had done it on purpose."

"After that I understand you knelt down beside your wife's body and prayed in silence."

"Yes, Sir. That was a rather cunning device that occurred to me on the spur of the moment. I realized that everyone knew me as a believer in Christianity. But while I was making a pretence of praying, I was in fact carefully calculating what attitude to adopt."

"So you were absolutely convinced that what you had done was on purpose?"

"I was. But I realized at once that I should be able to pretend it had been an accident."

"And why did you think it had been on purpose?"

"I had lost all sense of judgement."

"Did you think you'd succeeded in giving the impression it was an accident?"

"Yes, though when I thought about it afterwards it made my flesh creep. I pretended as convincingly as I could to be grief-stricken, but if there'd been just one really sharp-witted person about, he'd have realized right away that I was only acting. Well, that evening I decided that there was no good reason why I should not be acquitted; I told myself very calmly that there wasn't a shred of material evidence against me. To be sure, everyone knew how badly I got on with my wife, but if I persisted in saying that it was an accident, no one could prove the contrary. Going over in my mind everything that had happened, I saw that my wife's death could be explained very plausibly as an accident.

"And then a strange question came to my mind: why did I myself believe that it had not been an accident? To be sure, the previous night I had thought about killing her, but might it not be that very fact which now caused me to think of my act as deliberate? Gradually I came to the point that I myself did not know what actually had happened! At that I became very happy—almost unbearably happy. I wanted to shout at the top of my lungs."

"Because you had come to consider it an accident?"

"No, that I can't say: because I no longer had the slightest idea whether it had been intentional or not. So I decided that my best way of being acquitted would be to make a clean breast of everything. Rather than deceive myself and everyone else by saying it was an accident, why not be completely honest and say I did not know what happened? I cannot declare it was a mistake; on the other hand I can't admit it was intentional. In fact, I can plead neither 'guilty' nor 'not guilty'."

Han was silent. The judge, too, remained silent for a long moment before saying softly, reflectively:

"I believe that what you have told me is true. Just one more question; do you not feel the slightest sorrow for your wife's death?"

"None at all! Even when I hated my wife most bitterly in the past, I never could have imagined I would feel such happiness in talking about her death."

"Very well," said the judge. "You may stand down."

Han silently lowered his head and left the room. Feeling strangely moved, the judge reached for his pen. On the document which lay on the table he wrote down the words, "Not Guilty."

*Junichiro Tanizaki* (1886–1965) *was a brilliant, unconventional novelist who had a worldwide reputation. An admirer of Poe, his early works displayed an obsession with diabolism and masochism. He also wrote a small group of crime stories, "The Thief" being the only one we have in English. As he matured, his work revealed a deep appreciation of Japanese art and traditions, but he never lost his sensuous style. His best known work is* The Makioka Sisters *(1948, trans. 1957), a lengthy novel about the lives of four daughters of an old Osaka family, which was recently made into a highly successful film.*

*Many of Tanizaki's novels have been translated into English.* A Springtime Case *(1915, trans. 1927) and* The Key *(1956, trans. 1961), although not crime novels, contain enough crime fiction elements to engage the interest of mystery fans. An excellent selection of his short stories are translated in* Seven Japansese Tales *(1963).*

# The Thief

## by JUNICHIRO TANIZAKI

TRANSLATED BY HOWARD HIBBETT

It was years ago, at the school where I was preparing for Tokyo
Imperial University.

My dormitory roommates and I used to spend a lot of time at
what we called "candlelight study" (there was very little studying to
it), and one night, long after lights-out, the four of us were doing
just that, huddled around a candle talking on and on.

I recall that we were having one of our confused, heated
arguments about love—a problem of great concern to us in those
days. Then, by a natural course of development, the conversation
turned to the subject of crime: we found ourselves talking about
such things as swindling, theft, and murder.

"Of all crimes, the one we're most likely to commit is murder."
It was Higuchi, the son of a well-known professor, who declared
this. "But I don't believe I'd ever steal—I just couldn't do it. I think
I could be friends with any other kind of person, but a thief seems to
belong to a different species." A shadow of distaste darkened his
handsome features. Somehow that frown emphasized his good
looks.

"I hear there's been a rash of stealing in the dormitory lately."
This time it was Hirata who spoke. "Isn't that so?" he asked, turning
to Nakamura, our other roommate.

"Yes, and they say it's one of the students."

"How do they know?" I asked.

"Well, I haven't heard all the details—" Nakamura dropped his
voice to a confidential whisper. "But it's happened so often it must
be an inside job."

"Not only that," Higuchi put in, "one of the fellows in the north
wing was just going into his room the other day when somebody
pushed the door open from the inside, caught him with a hard slap
in the face, and ran away down the hall. He chased after him, but
by the time he got to the bottom of the stairs the other one was out
of sight. Back in his room, he found his trunk and bookshelves in a
mess, which proves it was the thief."

"Did he see his face?"

"No, it all happened too fast, but he says he looked like one of
us, the way he was dressed. Apparently he ran down the hall with
his coat pulled up over his head—the one thing sure is that his coat
had a wisteria crest."

"A wisteria crest?" said Hirata. "You can't prove anything by
that." Maybe it was only my imagination, but I thought he flashed a
suspicious look at me. At the same moment I felt that I instinctively
made a wry face, since my own family crest is a wisteria design. It
was only by chance that I wasn't wearing my crested coat that night.

"If he's one of us it won't be easy to catch him. Nobody wants to
believe there's a thief among us." I was trying to get over my
embarrassment because of that moment of weakness.

"No, they'll get him in a couple of days," Higuchi said
emphatically. His eyes were sparkling. "This is a secret, but they say

he usually steals things in the dressing room of the bathhouse, and for two or three days now the proctors have been keeping watch. They hide overhead and look down through a little hole."

"Oh? Who told you that?" Nakamura asked.

"One of the proctors. But don't go around talking about it."

"If *you* know so much, the thief probably knows it too!" said Hirata, looking disgusted.

Here I must explain that Hirata and I were not on very good terms. In fact, by that time we barely tolerated each other. I say "we," but it was Hirata who had taken a strong dislike to me. According to a friend of mine, he once remarked scornfully that I wasn't what everyone seemed to think I was, that he'd had a chance to see through me. And again: "I'm sick of him. He'll never be a friend of mine. It's only out of pity that I have anything to do with him."

He only said such things behind my back; I never heard them from him directly, though it was obvious that he loathed me. But it wasn't in my nature to demand an explanation. "If there's something wrong with me he ought to say so," I told myself. "If he doesn't have the kindness to tell me what it is, or if he thinks I'm not worth bothering with, then I won't think of *him* as a friend either." I felt a little lonely when I thought of his contempt for me, but I didn't really worry about it.

Hirata had an admirable physique and was the very type of masculinity that our school prides itself on, while I was skinny and pale and high-strung. There was something basically incompatible about us: I had to resign myself to the fact that we lived in separate worlds. Furthermore, Hirata was a judo expert of high rank, and displayed his muscles as if to say: "Watch out, or I'll give you a thrashing!" Perhaps it seemed cowardly of me to take such a meek attitude toward him, and no doubt I *was* afraid of his physical strength; but fortunately I was quite indifferent to matters of trivial pride or prestige. "I don't care how contemptuous the other fellow is; as long as I can go on believing in myself I don't need to feel bitter toward him." That was how I made up my mind, and so I was able to match Hirata's arrogance with my own cool magnanimity. I even told one of the other boys: "I can't help it if Hirata doesn't understand me, but I appreciate his good points anyway." And I actually believed it. I never considered myself a coward. I was even rather conceited, thinking I must be a person of noble character to be able to praise Hirata from the bottom of my heart.

"A wisteria crest?" That night, when Hirata cast his sudden glance at me, the malicious look in his eyes set my nerves on edge. What could that look possibly mean? Did he know that my family crest was wisteria? Or did I take it that way simply because of my own private feelings? If Hirata suspected *me*, how was I to handle the situation? Perhaps I should laugh good-naturedly and say: "Then I'm under suspicion too, because I have the same crest." If the others laughed along wth me, I'd be all right. But suppose one of them, say Hirata, only began looking grimmer and grimmer— what then? When I visualized that scene I couldn't very well speak out impulsively.

It sounds foolish to worry about such a thing, but during that brief silence all sorts of thoughts raced through my mind. "In this kind of situation what difference is there, really, between an innocent man and an actual criminal?" But then I felt that I was experiencing a criminal's anxiety and isolation. Until a moment ago I had been one of their friends, one of the elite of our famous school. But now, if only in my own mind, I was an outcast. It was absurd, but I suffered from my inability to confide in them. I was uneasy about Hirata's slightest mood—Hirata who was supposed to be my equal.

"A thief seems to belong to a different species." Higuchi had probably said this casually enough, but now his words echoed ominously in my mind.

"A thief belongs to a different species. . . ." A thief! What a detestable name to be called! I suppose what makes a thief different from other men is not so much his criminal act itself as his effort to hide it at all costs, the strain of trying to put it out of his mind, the dark fears that he can never confess. And now I was becoming enshrouded by that darkness. I was trying not to believe that I was under suspicion; I was worrying about fears that I could not admit to my closest friend. Of course it must have been because Higuchi trusted me that he told us what he'd heard from the proctor. "Don't go around talking about it," he had said, and I was glad. But why should I feel glad? I thought. After all, Higuchi has never suspected me. Somehow I began to wonder about his motive for telling us.

It also struck me that if even the most virtuous person has criminal tendencies, maybe I wasn't the only one who imagined the possibility of being a thief. Maybe the others were experiencing a little of the same discomfort, the same elation. If so, then Higuchi, who had been singled out by the proctor to share his secret, must have felt very proud. Among the four of us it was he who was most trusted, he who was thought least likely to belong to that "other species." And if he won that trust because he came from a wealthy family and was the son of a famous professor, then I could hardly avoid envying him. Just as his social status improved his moral character, so my own background—I was acutely conscious of being a scholarship student, the son of a poor farmer—debased mine. For me to feel a kind of awe in his presence had nothing to do with whether or not I was a thief. We *did* belong to different species. I felt that the more he trusted me, with his frank, open attitude, the more the gulf between us deepened. The more friendly we tried to be, joking with each other in apparent intimacy, gossiping and laughing together, the more the distance between us increased. There was nothing I could do about it.

For a long time afterward I worried about whether or not I ought to wear that coat of mine with the "wisteria crest." Perhaps if I wore it around nonchalantly no one would pay any attention. But suppose they looked at me as much as to say: "Ah, he's wearing it!" Some would suspect me, or try to suppress their doubts of me, or feel sorry for me because I was under suspicion. If I became embarrassed and uneasy not only with Hirata and Higuchi but with all the students, and if I then felt obliged to put my coat away, that would seem even more sinister. What I dreaded was not the bare fact of being suspect, but all the unpleasant emotions that would be stirred up in others. If I were to cause doubt in other people's minds I would create a barrier between myself and those who had always been my friends. Even theft itself was not as ugly as the suspicions that would be aroused by it. No one would want to think of me as a thief: as long as it hadn't been proved, they'd want to go on associating with me as freely as ever, forcing themselves to trust me. Otherwise, what would friendship mean? Thief or not, I might be guilty of a worse sin than stealing from a friend: the sin of spoiling a friendship. Sowing seeds of doubt about myself was criminal. It *was* worse than stealing. If I were a prudent, clever thief—no, I mustn't put it that way—if I were a thief with the least bit of conscience and consideration for other people, I'd try to keep my friendships untarnished, try to be open with my friends, treat them with a sincerity and warmth that I need never be ashamed of, while carrying out my thefts in secrecy. Perhaps I'd be what people call "a brazen thief," but if you look at it from the thief's point of view, it's the most honest attitude to take. "It's true that I steal, but it's equally true that I value my friends," such a man would say. "That is typical of a thief, that's why he belongs to a different species." Anyhow, when I started thinking that way, I couldn't help becoming more and more aware of the distance between me and my friends. Before I knew it I felt like a full-fledged thief.

One day I mustered up my courage and wore the crested coat out on the school grounds. I happened to meet Nakamura, and we began walking along together.

"By the way," I remarked, "I hear they haven't caught the thief yet."

"That's right," Nakamura answered, looking away.

"Why not? Couldn't they trap him at the bathhouse?"

"He didn't show up there again, but you still hear about lots of things being stolen in other places. They say the proctors called Higuchi in the other day and gave him the devil for letting their plan leak out."

"Higuchi?" I felt the color drain from my face.

"Yes. . . ." He sighed painfully, and a tear rolled down his cheek. "You've got to forgive me! I've kept it from you till now, but I think you ought to know the truth. You won't like this, but you're the one the proctors suspect. I hate to talk about it—I've never suspected you for a minute. I believe in you. And because I believe in you, I just had to tell you. I hope you won't hold it against me."

"Thanks for telling me. I'm grateful to you." I was almost in tears myself, but at the same time I thought: "It's come at last!" As much as I dreaded it, I'd been expecting this day to arrive.

"Let's drop the subject," said Nakamura, to comfort me. "I feel better now that I've told you."

"But we can't put it out of our minds just because we hate to talk about it. I appreciate your kindness, but I'm not the only one who's been humiliated—I've brought shame on you too, as my friend. The mere fact that I'm under suspicion makes me unworthy of friendship. Any way you look at it, my reputation is ruined. Isn't that so? I imagine you'll turn your back on me too."

"I swear I never will—and I don't think you've brought any shame on me." Nakamura seemed alarmed by my reproachful tone. "Neither does Higuchi. They say he did his best to defend you in front of the proctors. He told them he'd doubt himself before he doubted you."

"But they still suspect me, don't they? There's no use trying to spare my feelings. Tell me everything you know. I'd rather have it that way."

Then Nakamura hesitantly explained: "Well, it seems the proctors get all kinds of tips. Ever since Higuchi talked too much that night there haven't been any more thefts at the bathhouse, and that's why they suspect you."

"But I wasn't the only one who heard him!"—I didn't say this, but the thought occurred to me immediately. It made me feel even more lonely and wretched.

"But how did they know Higuchi told us? There were only the four of us that night, so if nobody else knew it, and if you and Higuchi trust me—"

"You'll have to draw your own conclusions," Nakamura said, with an imploring look. "You know who it is. He's misjudged you, but I don't want to criticize him."

A sudden chill came over me. I felt as if Hirata's eyes were glaring into mine.

"Did you talk to him about me?"

"Yes. . . . But I hope you realize that it isn't easy, since I'm his friend as well as yours. In fact, Higuchi and I had a long argument with him last night, and he says he's leaving the dormitory. So I have to lose one friend on account of another."

I took Nakamura's hand and gripped it hard. "I'm grateful for friends like you and Higuchi," I said, tears streaming from my eyes. Nakamura cried too. For the first time in my life I felt that I was really experiencing the warmth of human compassion. This was what I had been searching for while I was tormented by my sense of helpless isolation. No matter how vicious a thief I might be, I could never steal anything from Nakamura.

After a while I said: "To tell you the truth, I'm not worth the trouble I'm causing you. I can't stand by in silence and see you two lose such a good friend because of someone like me. Even though he doesn't trust me, I still respect him. He's a far better man than I am. I recognize his value as well as anyone. So why don't I move out instead, if it's come to that? Please—let *me* go, and you three can keep on living together. Even if I'm alone I'll feel better about it."

"But there's no reason for you to leave," said Nakamura, his voice charged with emotion. "I recognize his good points too, but you're the one that's being persecuted. I won't side with him when it's so unfair. If *you* leave, *we* ought to leave too. You know how stubborn he is—once he's made up his mind to go he's not apt to change it. Why not let him do as he pleases? We might as well wait for him to come to his senses and apologize. That shouldn't take very long anyway."

"But he'll never come back to apologize. He'll go on hating me forever."

Nakamura seemed to assume that I felt resentful toward Hirata. "Oh, I don't think so," he said quickly. "He'll stick to his word—that's both his strength and his weakness—but once he knows he's wrong he'll come and apologize, and make a clean breast of it. That's one of the likable things about him."

"It would be fine if he did . . . ," I said thoughtfully. "He may come back to you, but I don't believe he'll ever make friends with me again. . . . But you're right, he's really likable. I only wish he liked me too."

Nakamura put his hand on my shoulder as if to protect his poor friend, as we plodded listlessly along on the grass. It was evening and a light mist hung over the school grounds: we seemed to be on an island surrounded by endless gray seas. Now and then a few students walking the other way would glance at me and go on. They already know, I thought; they're ostracizing me. I felt an overwhelming loneliness.

That night Hirata seemed to have changed his mind; he showed no intention of moving. But he refused to speak to us—even to Higuchi and Nakamura. Yet for me to leave at this stage was impossible, I decided. Not only would I be disregarding the kindness of my friends, I would be making myself seem all the more guilty. I ought to wait a little longer.

"Don't worry," my two friends were forever telling me. "As soon as they catch him the whole business will clear up." But even after another week had gone by, the criminal was still at large and the thefts were as frequent as ever. At last even Nakamura and Higuchi lost some money and a few books.

"Well, you two finally got it, didn't you? But I have a feeling the rest of us won't be touched." I remember Hirata's taunting look as he made this sarcastic remark.

After supper Nakamura and Higuchi usually went to the library, and Hirata and I were left to confront each other. I found this so uncomfortable that I began spending my evenings away from the dormitory too, either going to the library or taking long walks. One night around nine-thirty I came back from a walk and looked into our study. Oddly enough, Hirata wasn't there, nor did the others seem to be back yet. I went to look in our bedroom, but it was empty too. Then I went back to the study and over to Hirata's desk. Quietly I opened his drawer and ferreted out the registered letter that had come to him from his home a few days ago. Inside the letter were three ten-yen money orders, one of which I leisurely removed and put in my pocket. I pushed the drawer shut again and sauntered out into the hall. Then I went down to the yard, cut across the tennis court, and headed for the dark weedy hollow where I always buried the things I stole. But at that moment someone yelled: "Thief!" and flew at me from behind, knocking me down with a blow to my head. It was Hirata.

"Come on, let's have it! Let's see what you stuck in your pocket!"

"All right, all right, you don't have to shout like that," I answered calmly, smiling at him. "I admit I stole your money order. If you ask for it I'll give it back to you, and if you tell me to come with you I'll go anywhere you say. So we understand each other, don't we? What more do you want?"

Hirata seemed to hesitate, but soon began furiously raining blows on my face. Somehow the pain was not wholly unpleasant. I felt suddenly relieved of the staggering burden I had been carrying.

"There's no use beating me up like this, when I fell right into your trap for you. I made that mistake because you were so sure of yourself—I thought: 'Why the devil can't I steal from *him*?' But now you've found me out, so that's all there is to it. Later on we'll laugh about it together."

I tried to shake Hirata's hand good-naturedly, but he grabbed me by the collar and dragged me off toward our room. That was the only time Hirata seemed contemptible in my eyes.

"Hey, you fellows, I've caught the thief! You can't say I was taken in by him!" Hirata swaggered into our room and shoved me down in front of Nakamura and Higuchi, who were back from the library. Hearing the commotion, the other boys in the dormitory came swarming around our doorway.

"Hirata's right!" I told my two friends, picking myself up from the floor. "I'm the thief." I tried to speak in my normal tone, as casually as ever, but I realized that my face had gone pale.

"I suppose you hate me," I said to them. "Or else you're ashamed of me. . . . You're both honest, but you're certainly gullible. Haven't I been telling you the truth over and over again? I even said: 'I'm not the person you think I am. Hirata's the man to trust. He'll never be taken in.' But you didn't understand. I told you: 'Even if you become friendly with Hirata again, he'll never make friends with *me*!' I went as far as to say: 'I know better than anyone what a fine fellow Hirata is!' Isn't that so? I've never lied to you, have I? You may ask why I didn't come out and tell you the whole truth. You probably think I was deceiving you after all. But try looking at it from my position. I'm sorry, but stealing is one thing I can't control. Still, I didn't like to deceive you, so I told you the truth in a roundabout way. I couldn't be any more honest than that—it's your fault for not taking my hints. Maybe you think I'm just being perverse, but I've never been more serious. You'll probably ask why I don't quit stealing, if I'm so anxious to be honest. But that's not a fair question. You see, I was born a thief. I tried to be as sincere as I could with you under the circumstances. There was nothing else I could do. Even then my conscience bothered me—didn't I ask you to let *me* move out, instead of Hirata? I wasn't trying to fool you, I really wanted to do it for your sake. It's true that I stole from you, but it's also true that I'm your friend. I appeal to your friendship: I want you to understand that even a thief has feelings."

Nakamura and Higuchi stood there in silence, blinking with astonishment.

"Well, I can see you think I've got a lot of nerve. You just don't understand me. I guess it can't be helped, since you're of a different species." I smiled to conceal my bitterness, and added: "But since I'm your friend I'll warn you that this isn't the last time a thing like this will happen. So be on your guard! You two made friends with a thief because of your gullibility. You're likely to run into trouble when you go out in the world. Maybe you get better grades in school, but Hirata is a better man. You can't fool Hirata!"

When I singled him out for praise, Hirata made a wry face and looked away. At that moment he seemed strangely ill at ease.

Many years have passed since then. I became a professional thief and have been often behind bars; yet I cannot forget those memories—especially my memories of Hirata. Whenever I am about to commit a crime I see his face before me. I see him swaggering about as haughtily as ever, sneering at me: "Just as I suspected!" Yes, he was a man of character with great promise. But the world is mysterious. My prediction that the naïve Higuchi would "run into trouble" was wrong: partly through his father's influence, he has had a brilliant career—traveling abroad, earning a doctoral degree, and today holding a high position in the Ministry of Railways. Meanwhile nobody knows what has become of Hirata. It's no wonder we think life is unpredictable.

I assure my reader that this account is true. I have not written a single dishonest word here. And, as I hoped Nakamura and Higuchi would, I hope you will believe that delicate moral scruples can exist in the heart of a thief like me.

But perhaps you won't believe me either. Unless of course (if I may be pardoned for suggesting it) you happen to belong to my own species.

*Ryunosuke Akutagawa (1892–1927) is the best known of all Japanese short story writers. His worldwide reputation resulted from the huge success of Kurosawa's film* Rashomon *(1950), which was based on two stories by Akutagawa, "Rashomon" and "In a Grove." The film, Japan's first internationally acclaimed motion picture, generated interest in Akutagawa and led to the translation of his stories into many languages.*

*In much of his fiction, Akutagawa delves into the macabre. He also wrote some satirical and a few autobiographical pieces. His finest stories, however, are reinterpretations of historical tales. One of these is "In a Grove," an old tale that he converted into a series of statements made at a murder trial by seven witnesses, three of whom are principals in the case. The statements are conflicting, and what actually happened at the scene of the crime is left for the reader to decide.*

*Critics have praised Akutagawa for his intellectual and highly polished prose style. A sensitive man who was plagued by poor health and other personal problems, he ended his life by taking a fatal dose of veronal at the age of thirty-five.*

*Translations of Akutagawa's stories are widely available. The most accessible collections in English are* Rashomon and Other Stories *(1952),* Japanese Short Stories *(1961), and* Exotic Japanese Stories *(1964).*

# In a Grove

## by RYUNOSUKE AKUTAGAWA

### TRANSLATED BY TAKASHI KOJIMA

### THE TESTIMONY OF A WOODCUTTER QUESTIONED BY A HIGH POLICE COMMISSIONER

Yes, sir. Certainly, it was I who found the body. This morning, as usual, I went to cut my daily quota of cedars, when I found the body in a grove in a hollow in the mountains. The exact location? About 150 meters off the Yamashina stage road. It's an out-of-the-way grove of bamboo and cedars.

The body was lying flat on its back dressed in a bluish silk kimono and a wrinkled head-dress of the Kyoto style. A single sword-stroke had pierced the breast. The fallen bamboo-blades around it were stained with bloody blossoms. No, the blood was no longer running. The wound had dried up, I believe. And also, a gad-fly was stuck fast there, hardly noticing my footsteps.

You ask me if I saw a sword or any such thing?

No, nothing, sir. I found only a rope at the root of a cedar near by. And . . . well, in addition to a rope, I found a comb. That was all. Apparently he must have made a battle of it before he was murdered, because the grass and fallen bamboo-blades had been trampled down all around.

"A horse was near by?"

No, sir. It's hard enough for a man to enter, let alone a horse.

### THE TESTIMONY OF A TRAVELING BUDDHIST PRIEST QUESTIONED BY A HIGH POLICE COMMISSIONER

The time? Certainly, it was about noon yesterday, sir. The unfortunate man was on the road from Sekiyama to Yamashina. He was walking toward Sekiyama with a woman accompanying him on horseback, who I have since learned was his wife. A scarf hanging from her head hid her face from view. All I saw was the color of her clothes, a lilac-colored suit. Her horse was a sorrel with a fine mane. The lady's height? Oh, about four feet five inches. Since I am a Buddhist priest, I took little notice about her details. Well, the man was armed with a sword as well as a bow and arrows. And I remember that he carried some twenty odd arrows in his quiver.

Little did I expect that he would meet such a fate. Truly human life is as evanescent as the morning dew or a flash of lightning. My words are inadequate to express my sympathy for him.

### THE TESTIMONY OF A POLICEMAN QUESTIONED BY A HIGH POLICE COMMISSIONER

The man that I arrested? He is a notorious brigand called Tajomaru. When I arrested him, he had fallen off his horse. He was groaning on the bridge at Awataguchi. The time? It was in the early hours of last night. For the record, I might say that the other day I tried to arrest him, but unfortunately he escaped. He was wearing a dark blue silk kimono and a large plain sword. And, as you see, he got a bow and arrows somewhere. You say that this bow and these arrows look like the ones owned by the dead man? Then Tajomaru must be the murderer. The bow wound with leather strips, the black lacquered quiver, the seventeen arrows with hawk feathers—these were all in his possession I believe. Yes, sir, the horse is, as you say, a sorrel with a fine mane. A little beyond the stone bridge I found the horse grazing by the roadside, with his long rein dangling. Surely there is some providence in his having been thrown by the horse.

Of all the robbers prowling around Kyoto, this Tajomaru has given the most grief to the women in town. Last autumn a wife who came to the mountain back of the Pindora of the Toribe Temple, presumably to pay a visit, was murdered, along with a girl. It has been suspected that it was his doing. If this criminal murdered the man, you cannot tell what he may have done with the man's wife. May it please your honor to look into this problem as well.

### THE TESTIMONY OF AN OLD WOMAN QUESTIONED BY A HIGH POLICE COMMISSIONER

Yes, sir, that corpse is the man who married my daughter. He does not come from Kyoto. He was a samurai in the town of Kokufu in the province of Wakasa. His name was Kanazawa no Takehiko, and his age was twenty-six. He was of a gentle disposition, so I am sure he did nothing to provoke the anger of others.

My daughter? Her name is Masago, and her age is nineteen. She is a spirited, fun-loving girl, but I am sure she has never known any man except Takehiko. She has a small, oval, dark-complected face with a mole at the corner of her left eye.

Yesterday Takehiko left for Wakasa with my daughter. What bad luck it is that things should have come to such a sad end! What has become of my daughter? I am resigned to giving up my son-in-law as lost, but the fate of my daughter worries me sick. For heaven's sake leave no stone unturned to find her. I hate that robber Tajomaru, or whatever his name is. Not only my son-in-law, but my daughter . . . (Her later words were drowned in tears.)

## TAJOMARU'S CONFESSION

I killed him, but not her. Where's she gone? I can't tell. Oh, wait a minute. No torture can make me confess what I don't know. Now things have come to such a head, I won't keep anything from you.

Yesterday a little past noon I met that couple. Just then a puff of wind blew, and raised her hanging scarf, so that I caught a glimpse of her face. Instantly it was again covered from my view. That may have been one reason; she looked like a Bodhisattva. At that moment I made up my mind to capture her even if I had to kill her man.

Why? To me killing isn't a matter of such great consequence as you might think. When a woman is captured, her man has to be killed anyway. In killing, I use the sword I wear at my side. Am I the only one who kills people? You, you don't use your swords. You kill people with your power, with your money. Sometimes you kill them on the pretext of working for their good. It's true they don't bleed. They are in the best of health, but all the same you've killed them. It's hard to say who is a greater sinner, you or me. (An ironical smile.)

But it would be good if I could capture a woman without killing her man. So, I made up my mind to capture her, and do my best not to kill him. But it's out of the question on the Yamashina stage road. So I managed to lure the couple into the mountains.

It was quite easy. I became their traveling companion, and I told them there was an old mound in the mountain over there, and that I had dug it open and found many mirrors and swords. I went on to tell them I'd buried the things in a grove behind the mountain, and that I'd like to sell them at a low price to anyone who would care to have them. Then . . . you see, isn't greed terrible? He was beginning to be moved by my talk before he knew it. In less than half an hour they were driving their horse toward the mountain with me.

When he came in front of the grove, I told them that the treasures were buried in it, and I asked them to come and see. The man had no objection—he was blinded by greed. The woman said she would wait on horseback. It was natural for her to say so, at the sight of a thick grove. To tell you the truth, my plan worked just as I wished, so I went into the grove with him, leaving her behind alone.

The grove is only bamboo for some distance. About fifty yards ahead there's a rather open clump of cedars. It was a convenient spot for my purpose. Pushing my way through the grove, I told him a plausible lie that the treasures were buried under the cedars. When I told him this, he pushed his laborious way toward the slender cedar visible through the grove. After a while the bamboo thinned out, and we came to where a number of cedars grew in a row. As soon as we got there, I seized him from behind. Because he was a trained, sword-bearing warrior, he was quite strong, but he was taken by surprise, so there was no help for him. I soon tied him up to the root of a cedar. Where did I get a rope? Thank heaven, being a robber, I had a rope with me, since I might have to scale a wall at any moment. Of course it was easy to stop him from calling out by gagging his mouth with fallen bamboo leaves.

When I disposed of him, I went to his woman and asked her to come and see him, because he seemed to have been suddenly taken sick. It's needless to say that this plan also worked well. The woman, her sedge hat off, came into the depths of the grove, where I led her by the hand. The instant she caught sight of her husband, she drew a small sword. I've never seen a woman of such violent temper. If I'd been off guard, I'd have got a thrust in my side. I dodged, but she kept on slashing at me. She might have wounded me deeply or killed me. But I'm Tajomaru. I managed to strike down her small sword without drawing my own. The most spirited woman is defenseless without a weapon. At last I could satisfy my desire for her without taking her husband's life.

Yes, . . . without taking his life. I had no wish to kill him. I was about to run away from the grove, leaving the woman behind in tears, when she frantically clung to my arm. In broken fragments of words, she asked that either her husband or I die. She said it was more trying than death to have her shame known to two men. She gasped out that she wanted to be the wife of whichever survived. Then a furious desire to kill him seized me. (Gloomy excitement.)

Telling you in this way, no doubt I seem a crueler man than you. But that's because you didn't see her face. Especially her burning eyes at that moment. As I saw her eye to eye, I wanted to make her my wife even if I were to be struck by lightning. I wanted to make her my wife . . . this single desire filled my mind. This was not only lust, as you might think. At that time if I'd had no other desire than lust, I'd surely not have minded knocking her down and running away. Then I wouldn't have stained my sword with his blood. But the moment I gazed at her face in the dark grove, I decided not to leave there without killing him.

But I didn't like to resort to unfair means to kill him. I untied him and told him to cross swords with me. (The rope that was found at the root of the cedar is the rope I dropped at the time.) Furious with anger, he drew his thick sword. And quick as thought, he sprang at me ferociously, without speaking a word. I needn't tell you how our fight turned out. The twenty-third stroke . . . please remember this. I'm impressed with this fact still. Nobody under the sun has ever clashed swords with me twenty strokes. (A cheerful smile.)

When he fell, I turned toward her, lowering my blood-stained sword. But to my great astonishment she was gone. I wondered to where she had run away. I looked for her in the clump of cedars. I listened, but heard only a groaning sound from the throat of the dying man.

As soon as we started to cross swords, she may have run away through the grove to call for help. When I thought of that, I decided it was a matter of life and death to me. So, robbing him of his sword, and bow and arrows, I ran out to the mountain road. There I found her horse still grazing quietly. It would be a mere waste of words to tell you the later details, but before I entered town I had already parted with the sword. That's all my confession. I know that my head will be hung in chains anyway, so put me down for the maximum penalty. (A defiant attitude.)

### The Confession of a Woman Who Has
### Come to the Shimizu Temple

That man in the blue silk kimono, after forcing me to yield to him, laughed mockingly as he looked at my bound husband. How horrified my husband must have been! But no matter how hard he struggled in agony, the rope cut into him all the more tightly. In spite of myself I ran stumblingly toward his side. Or rather I tried to run toward him, but the man instantly knocked me down. Just at that moment I saw an indescribable light in my husband's eyes. Something beyond expression . . . his eyes make me shudder even now. That instantaneous look of my husband, who couldn't speak a word, told me all his heart. The flash in his eyes was neither anger nor sorrow . . . only a cold light, a look of loathing. More struck by the look in his eyes than by the blow of the thief, I called out in spite of myself and fell unconscious.

In the course of time I came to, and found that the man in blue silk was gone. I saw only my husband still bound to the root of the cedar. I raised myself from the bamboo-blades with difficulty, and looked into his face; but the expression in his eyes was just the same as before.

Beneath the cold contempt in his eyes, there was hatred. Shame, grief, and anger . . . I don't know how to express my heart at that time. Reeling to my feet, I went up to my husband.

"Takejiro," I said to him, "since things have come to this pass, I cannot live with you. I'm determined to die, . . . but you must die, too. You saw my shame. I can't leave you alive as you are."

This was all I could say. Still he went on gazing at me with loathing and contempt. My heart breaking, I looked for his sword. It must have been taken by the robber. Neither his sword nor his bow and arrows were to be seen in the grove. But fortunately my small sword was lying at my feet. Raising it over head, once more I said, "Now give me your life. I'll follow you right away."

When he heard these words, he moved his lips with difficulty. Since his mouth was stuffed with leaves, of course his voice could not be heard at all. But at a glance I understood his words. Despising me, his look said only, "Kill me." Neither conscious nor unconscious, I stabbed the small sword through the lilac-colored kimono into his breast.

Again at this time I must have fainted. By the time I managed to look up, he had already breathed his last—still in bonds. A streak of sinking sunlight streamed through the clump of cedars and bamboos, and shone on his pale face. Gulping down my sobs, I untied the rope from his dead body. And . . . and what has become of me since I have no more strength to tell you. Anyway I hadn't the strength to die. I stabbed my own throat with the small sword, I threw myself into a pond at the foot of the mountain, and I tried to kill myself in many ways. Unable to end my life, I am still living in dishonor. (A lonely smile.) Worthless as I am, I must have been forsaken even by the most merciful Kwannon. I killed my own husband. I was violated by the robber. Whatever can I do? Whatever can I . . . I . . . (Gradually, violent sobbing.)

## The Story of the Murdered Man, as Told
### through a Medium

After violating my wife, the robber, sitting there, began to speak comforting words to her. Of course I couldn't speak. My whole body was tied fast to the root of a cedar. But meanwhile I winked at her many times, as much as to say "Don't believe the robber". I wanted to convey some such meaning to her. But my wife, sitting dejectedly on the bamboo leaves, was looking hard at her lap. To all appearance, she was listening to his words. I was agonized by jealousy. In the meantime the robber went on with his clever talk, from one subject to another. The robber finally made his bold, brazen proposal. "Once your virture is stained, you won't get along well with your husband, so won't you be my wife instead? It's my love for you that made me be violent toward you."

While the criminal talked, my wife raised her face as if in a trance. She had never looked so beautiful as at that moment. What did my beautiful wife say in answer to him while I was sitting bound there? I am lost in space, but I have never thought of her answer without burning with anger and jealousy. Truly she said, . . . "Then take me away with you wherever you go."

This is not the whole of her sin. If that were all, I would not be tormented so much in the dark. When she was going out of the grove as if in a dream, her hand in the robber's, she suddenly turned pale, and pointed at me tied to the root of the cedar, and said, "Kill him! I cannot marry you as long as he lives." "Kill him!" she cried many times, as if she had gone crazy. Even now these words threaten to blow me headlong into the bottomless abyss of darkness. Has such a hateful thing come out of a human mouth ever before? Have such cursed words ever struck a human ear, even once? Even once such a . . . (A sudden cry of scorn.) At these words the robber himself turned pale. "Kill him," she cried, clinging to his arms. Looking hard at her, he answered neither yes nor no. . . . but hardly had I thought about his answer before she had been knocked down into the bamboo leaves. (Again a cry of scorn.) Quietly folding his arms, he looked at me and said, "What will you do with her? Kill her or save her? You have only to nod. Kill her?" For these words alone I would like to pardon his crime.

While I hesitated, she shrieked and ran into the depths of the grove. The robber instantly snatched at her, but he failed even to grasp her sleeve.

After she ran away, he took up my sword, and my bow and arrows. With a single stroke he cut one of my bonds. I remember his mumbling, "My fate is next." Then he disappeared from the grove. All was silent after that. No, I heard someone crying. Untying the rest of my bonds, I listened carefully, and I noticed that it was my own crying. (Long silence.)

I raised my exhausted body from the root of the cedar. In front of me there was shining the small sword which my wife had dropped. I took it up and stabbed it into my breast. A bloody lump rose to my mouth, but I didn't feel any pain. When my breast grew cold, everything was as silent as the dead in their graves. What profound silence! Not a single bird-note was heard in the sky over this grave in the hollow of the mountains. Only a lonely light lingered on the cedars and mountain. By and by the light gradually grew fainter, till the cedars and bamboo were lost to view. Lying there, I was enveloped in deep silence.

Then someone crept up to me. I tried to see who it was. But darkness had already been gathering round me. Someone . . . that someone drew the small sword softly out of my breast in its invisible hand. At the same time once more blood flowed into my mouth. And once and for all I sank down into the darkness of space.

*Tatsuzo Ishikawa* (1905–1984) *was a popular novelist who earned a reputation as an acute observer of the social scene. His first major success came with* The People (1935), *a novel about Japanese emigrants in Brazil. He produced a series of big-scale novels, each dealing with a social problem and usually advocating a common sense approach and gradual progress. His* Living Soldiers (1938) *presented such a realistic picture of the war in China that he found himself in trouble with authorities. Although not a crime writer, he often used crime elements in his work, as in "The Affair of the Arabesque Inlay," a depiction of Japan during the immediate postwar years.*

*Two of Ishikawa's novels have been translated into English. One,* Resistance at Forty-Eight (1956, trans. 1960), *tells about the mid-life crisis of a sensible, middle class man. The other is* Evil for Pleasure (1954, trans. 1972), *which comes close to being a crime novel. The hero is a man who spices his otherwise dull life with petty crimes and mischief, until one day he commits a truly serious offense—murder.*

# The Affair of the Arabesque Inlay

## by TATSUZO ISHIKAWA

### TRANSLATED BY MAKOTO MOMOI
### AND JAY GLUCK

*Dear Sir:*
*Reference is made to your latest inquiry after our investigation into the present whereabouts and recent activities of one Mr. Wu Kao-chih.*

*We hereby take great pleasure to inform you of the results of our inquiries to date.*

*It is also sincerely requested that you would kindly understand that our report as yet includes certain insufficiencies primarily due to the difficulty in establishing the present whereabouts of the person involved.*

*Yours Sincerely*

*(signed:) T. Torii*
*Chief of Torii Detective Agency*
*Encl: Report to date. T.T.*

Mr. Wu Kao-chih, of Chinese nationality; born Nanking, 1918. Father alleged to have been a noted trader by the name of Wu Hsiung-ta.

Mr. Wu Kao-chih studied economics in a university in Shanghai. Later he was brought to Japan by his father. Here he studied economics at Waseda University, as evidenced by the students' enrollment records of said University.

In 1937, the Lukowkiao Incident set off the Sino-Japanese War. However, Mr. Wu did not return home until 1938, upon his formal graduation from Waseda University.

After the war, early in 1946, he again came to Japan, allegedly making a quick fortune at smuggling and such activities by taking full advantage of his nationality.

In June, 1951, upon the signing of the San Francisco peace treaty, and resumption of Japanese authority over the affairs of Third Nationals and the subsequent decline in his business, he returned to China.

His subsequent whereabouts are unknown, except for August, 1953, when Yumiko Ueda, with whom he had maintained a special relationship while he was in Japan, received by mail an expensive English-made jewelry box. The parcel noted the origin as Nanking.

To our regret, further details are not available.

Judging from several old photos he left in Japan, he would seem to be five feet five inches or so in height, tending toward plumpness, of a gay disposition, and of Southern Chinese racial type.

According to information gathered from his acquaintances in Japan, we have drawn up an outline of his life and character as follows: During his entire three years in Japan as a student of the Economics Department of Waseda University, he rented a room in the home of Mr. Yasuhiro Arai, then a director of the Japan-Formosa Spinning Company. Regarding him, widow of Arai recalls, "Mr. Wu Kao-chih was a very steady student and pro-Japanese." She also said, "My husband was a good friend of the senior Mr. Wu. We invited young Wu to our house. Brought up in a good family, he was very polite and modest. But he also had progressive ideas—thinking that China should throw off her old ways and rebuild a new China which could cope with progress and the rest of the world."

Mrs. Arai's impression coincides with those of Wu's classmates. He remained a bachelor, and was strictly against the Chinese custom of early marriage.

In the Spring of 1938, upon his graduation from Waseda University, he returned to a China under Japanese military occupation. Further records of him from that date until 1946, when he revisited Japan, are unavailable due to lack of means of investigation from here. However, consolidating data from the testimonials of Yumiko Ueda and other people, the history we have reconstructed for him during the period in question is an extremely tragic one.

In December, 1937, the Japanese Army was pressing close to Nanking city from the east. Mr. Wu Kao-chih, then in Tokyo, had received no word from his family since November. After the fierce fighting on December 12 and 13, Nanking surrendered. The Japanese Army issued the formal declaration of the occupation of Nanking on December 17. Mr. Wu desperately wanted to know of his father, mother and sisters. He did all he could to find some means of returning home, but the severe restrictions which then prevailed allowed him no chance of exit from Japan—legal or illegal.

Late in March, 1938, he somehow managed to return to his homeland. In Nanking, he found only ashes and rubble where his father's office had been. His father's house was demolished. All possessions had been looted. No trace of his parents or sisters was found. He was told that tens of thousands of Nanking citizens had been massacred by the Japanese Army; then the corpses were buried in mass graves outside the city walls.

For almost half a year, Mr. Wu wandered around trying to locate—or at least to learn the whereabouts of the bodies of—his family. During that fruitless search, Mr. Wu's attitude toward life seems to have undergone a complete change. So, too, did his personal character.

From that time until his return to Japan in 1946, his activities are unknown. He is believed to have availed himself of the opportunities offered by the confusion of the war and to have established his financial position solidly. In 1946 Mr. Wu came to Japan, alone. First, settling himself in the so-called Nanking Street, of Chinatown, Yokohama, he started trading. Soon he moved to Tokyo, pocketing large profits through the importation of American luxury goods, Taiwan sugar and bananas. Black-marketing gasoline seems to have brought considerable money into his pockets.

He bought a fine house in Denen Chofu, hired secretaries, maids, drove a Cadillac—himself, no chauffeur. At night he frequented cabarets in the Ginza with his friends.

It was about February of 1950 that Yumiko Ueda got to know Mr. Wu. Yumiko was then thirty-two, had been working at Cabaret Tokyo from January 1950.

Yumiko Ueda was born on a farm in Kumagaya, Saitama Prefecture, the second daughter. Her father, Harukichi Ueda, died of illness in 1944. After finishing girls' high school in Kumagaya, she came to Tokyo to be a student nurse at the Central Red Cross Hospital. Later she became a nurse in the First National Hospital, where she worked for three years.

The relationship between Mr. Wu Kao-chih and Yumiko Ueda became regularized in 1950. Mr. Wu bought a house in Takaban-cho, for Yumiko and her child, providing a maid. But this relationship was brought to its conclusion as described in the following.

Our investigator interviewed Yumiko Ueda, who is now living at her brother's farm in Kumagaya. She told our investigator, "I first met him in the cabaret where I worked. He always brought a few friends with him. His Japanese and his manner were so natural that I could hardly believe he was a foreigner. He was a fine, clean-cut gentleman, generous with his money. He was perhaps at his most prosperous at that time. I overheard it said that he could make several hundred thousand yen selling an imported car to a Japanese."

One night one or two months after they first met, Wu was drinking sake at the cabaret. He looked at his watch, and murmured that he didn't realize it was so late. Yumiko unconsciously looked at her wrist watch and said, "Oh, it's just nine-sixteen."

Wu looked at her wrist—then stared at the watch as if to check its movement. "What are you gazing at?" Yumiko says she asked.

"It's very beautiful. May I see it closer?" he said and took her hand.

"No, it's only a cheap one. I'm ashamed," she reportedly answered.

"No, it's not at all cheap. It's a rather rare watch. Do you mind if I see its back?" He was unusually insistent, she recalls.

Yumiko took the watch off her wrist and handed it to Wu. He turned it over, closely examining the inlaid arabesque design of a little red flower. Then he returned it to her without a word.

Half an hour later, just before they left, Mr. Wu whispered into Yumiko's ear, "Yumiko-san, couldn't you sell me that watch for five thousand yen?"

Surprised, Yumiko hesitated.

"Maybe five thousand yen is too cheap? Will seven or eight thousand yen do? I must have that watch," he insisted.

"Why? It's just an old watch. You can buy any brand-new one you see," Yumiko said.

"Please think it over. I don't mind paying even ten thousand yen for it." And he left.

The next day, he came to the cabaret alone—which was unusual. He asked her about the watch. She sold it, agreeing to eight thousand yen—but when later she opened the envelope he had given her, she found ten one-thousand-yen notes.

Placing the watch in his vest pocket, Mr. Wu asked her: "Where did you buy this, Yumiko-san?"

"I was given it."

"Is that so? Well, may I ask who gave it to you?"

"It's a keep-sake of my dead parents."

"A keep-sake? Was your mother wearing this?"

"It was from my father."

"That's not true. This is a woman's watch."

"Yes, that's right."

"Let me guess. It must be your lover who bought this for you."

"Oh, it's such a trifle, let's forget it." She tried to change the subject, but Wu turned serious and started to tell her a story. He had a very intimate friend—a crazy collector of timepieces—whose collection included over fourteen or fifteen hundred old and new, Western and Oriental, watches and clocks. Wu had allegedly picked up some slight knowledge of watches from his friend. Wu told her that the watch was an extremely novel piece—not made in Switzerland, England, or America. Nor did it look Japanese. The design on the back side seemed Chinese, but the face was in the European style.

He wanted to know where it came from. Otherwise, he said, he could provide no clue to his friend's research—that was the general outline of Mr. Wu's story. Yumiko was taken in by the story. She confessed, "In fact, I don't know the details of its origin. I got it from a relative of mine who had been a soldier. It often goes out of order—It isn't a good watch—"

"Is that so? . . . a soldier gave it to you . . . I wish . . . well, if I could see him sometime . . . That soldier couldn't have been to, say . . . well, Korea? . . . Manchuria? . . . Singapore? Perhaps China? . . . I wonder . . ."

"Yes, he's been to China. During the war. And he returned—wounded in battle."

"Ah, I see . . . China!" He raised his voice a little. He smiled. His eyes glistened strangely.

After this Wu came to Yumiko's cabaret as often as twice a week. In addition to the usual tips, he began leaving special pocket money in her hands. Yumiko was naturally impressed by the fact that Mr. Wu was a bachelor, living in a big mansion.

Not long after, she was invited to accompany him on a business trip to the Osaka-Kobe area. It was a five-day trip with stopovers at the Takarazuka Hot-Spring and Kyoto Hotels. At this time they entered into their special relationship. Yumiko confessed to him that she had a child. Mr. Wu bought clothing material and other presents for the child. According to Yumiko, Mr. Wu Kao-chih was not of a demanding nature, never trying to monopolize her.

About a month after that trip Mr. Wu bought a new, though small, modern house in Takabancho. Yumiko moved from her shabby room in Asakusa-Tabaramachi, with her child, and hired a maid. In short, she became a mistress to Mr. Wu Kao-chih, a Chinese living in Japan.

Every month, she received fifty thousand yen as living expenses, besides occasional presents and extra money he gave her whenever he visited the house. Yumiko's life became comfortable. She quit the cabaret, but was still able to save over twenty thousand yen a month. Then one night Mr. Wu Kao-chih resumed the long-forgotten talk about her watch. It came as a great surprise to Yumiko, who had believed that Wu was interested in the watch for his collector friend.

It was a lie—a pious means to an end.

It seems that watch had, without any doubt, belonged to Wu's mother. His father had bought it for her on their twentieth wedding anniversary. The design, specially ordered by his father, precluded there being another like it in the world. Wu wanted to locate the person who had had the watch previously. Whoever gave it to Yumiko might know something about his parents and sisters, missing since the occupation of Nanking.

Mr. Wu also told Yumiko that he had to see the soldier who had given the watch to her. His real purpose in revisiting post-war Japan was not to make money but to find Japanese who knew the fate of his parents and sisters. He "had a hunch that some Japanese should know," he said, his face suddenly gone white.

Yumiko had no reason to refuse to cooperate with him, particularly as she was being provided for so generously, but a chill went down her back when she thought of how Wu had, as the ancient saying puts it, "attained the fact by sure steps."

She was thankful for all he had done for her and her child, whatever his real intention might have been. Yet she could not disclose the truth. What would happen if that soldier was the very person who had killed Wu's family? The soldier was none other than the father of her own child.

Yumiko confessed to our investigator that she had "only hatred and no obligation at all toward that soldier," but still she was unwilling to disclose his identity to Wu. Nevertheless, her past finally yielded to the power of her present. He was the father of her daughter; still, he was never her formal husband. On the other hand, though only a mistress, Yumiko felt a love and obligation toward Wu, sentiment that finally made her confess the name of her former lover.

Otojiro Haneda, registered domicile Odawara City, Kanagawa Prefecture. After finishing middle school, worked for Hakone Tozan Railway and at other jobs. In 1935, entered the army as a Private Second Class. In August, 1937, at the outbreak of the Sino-Japanese incident, went to China. By the time of the fall of Nanking, he was a corporal. In July, 1938, Cpl. Haneda received a wound in a guerilla mop-up—bone fractures of the left thigh and knee joint. Hospitalized in the army's Nanking Hospital, later returned to Japan. In the First Army Hospital met Yumiko Ueda, then assigned as a nurse.

After about a year, he was released from the hospital with a slightly crippled leg. Soon after, rented a room in Tokyo, where both lived together. In spring 1941, Yumiko gave birth to a girl.

Not long after the daughter's birth, Haneda left Tokyo for Odawara—with the excuse that he could find a better job there. Six months passed without a word. In the spring of 1942 Yumiko received a letter telling her that he had to marry another girl as the inevitable result of certain circumstances. In the letter was enclosed a three-hundred-yen check. Yumiko tried every way to locate Haneda, but failed.

As to the watch, Yumiko told Mr. Wu that she had received it while she was nursing Haneda in the First Army Hospital. He said that he bought it in a curio shop in Shanghai. Mr. Wu did not believe the story of Haneda. Rather he suspected that former Corporal Haneda had been among the troops occupying Nanking. It might be said to be the instinct of a son whose parents had been killed.

No sooner had Mr. Wu obtained the name of Haneda from Yumiko than he went straight to Odawara city. In five days he succeeded in locating Haneda. He seems to have spent a considerable amount of money in checking over the whole town through five Chinese residents of that city.

Otojiro Haneda was not living in Odawara. But Mr. Wu did locate Haneda's brother, who revealed Haneda's whereabouts as near Okachimachi, back in Tokyo. Haneda was dealing in black-market goods of the American occupation forces. He was living in a four-room house near Ueno, with wife and employees—but no children.

Mr. Wu was not so hasty as to call on Haneda at his house. He went to the shop Haneda was operating. First approaching as a customer, Mr. Wu was soon selling him imported articles—at prices considerably below market. Haneda was delighted. Haneda soon began to treat Mr. Wu as a trusted friend. Haneda did not see through Mr. Wu, who passed as a Japanese called Yoshizo Iwamoto.

They were soon on quite familiar terms. One night at a sake party Mr. Wu, alias Iwamoto, asked Haneda, "By the way, this may sound odd, but, don't you by any chance know a girl named Ueda Yumiko?"

Haneda was startled. "Anything happened to Yumiko?" he asked.

"No, nothing. But is she your wife?"

"No. Not my wife. But I lived with her for a while."

"Did you?—and, uh, you had a child, didn't you?"

"Yes, I did. Is . . . my child is all right?"

"Seems so. Seven or eight now, isn't she?"

"Maybe, eight or nine, by now. How on earth do you come to know them?"

"No, no, I don't really know them. Only, well, one of my friends is taking care of them. A few days ago—I was in his house— we talked about the Okachimachi Market. This woman suddenly asked me if I knew a man in the market called Haneda. I was surprised. She seems to have been working in the Cabaret Tokyo in the Ginza. But then I think she had already quit the place," said Wu, alias Iwamoto.

Soon after Otojiro Haneda went to the Cabaret Tokyo to find

Yumiko. He was directed to her new home. Luckily, Mr. Wu was not there.

The moment Yumiko faced Haneda, an old, almost forgotten, burning rancor welled up in her heart. She kept him standing on the stone floor of the entrance hall, never asking him to step inside.

"Hello, Yumiko. It's been long time—"

"What brought you here? I really wonder how you could even dare to come," she sputtered in rage.

"Of course, I have no face to come to you like this, but—I just wanted to see my child."

"Your child? Huh! You wouldn't really like to face the child you deserted, would you? You'd better leave."

"Don't talk like that. That time, well, I was in a tight squeeze. I apologize——" Haneda tried all the excuses and explanations he could muster. "You see," he said. "Well, as a matter of fact, I have given you so much trouble in bringing up the child—but if you agree, I would like to send her to the university—with my money. I mean, I am getting along fairly well now." He also added that he had no child with his present wife, who was willing to adopt his child by the former affair.

Yumiko was furious at his selfishness. She threatened him with a pair of *geta* she grabbed from the stone floor. He left without further argument. Yumiko did not say anything to Mr. Wu, as she feared giving him the wrong notion that she was continuing her old affair.

She received an anonymous parcel, obviously from Haneda, who, though, did not put his address on it—there was one hundred thousand yen inside. Unable to return it, she kept the money in the drawer of her wardrobe. A few days later a messenger brought a basket of fruit. She ignored the basket and returned the money with it.

Otojiro Haneda tried to get his child back through various means—money, presents—all of which failed. In consequence he apparently began to consider some drastic action to achieve his end. But it took another month before he could finally carry it out.

In the meantime, Mr. Wu was handling Haneda in his way. Practically all of Haneda's business now depended on "Iwamoto."

It was precisely the way Mr. Wu had approached Yumiko, made her his own, and explored the secret of the watch—the way only a persistent Chinese could pursue.

One night "Iwamoto" took Haneda to Atami and got him drunk. Making sure that he was tight enough, Iwamoto—alias Mr. Wu Kao-chih—asked, "You always wear khaki pants. You've been in the army?"

"Of course.—Who's asking me? I am a corporal—decorated—the Order of the Golden Kite—" Haneda said in drunken pride.

"Well then—you were crippled in the leg—an honorable wound?"

"That's right—mortar shell got me. Almost lost a leg——"

"Where did you go? South?"

"Central China. From there as far as Nanking. Had a real rough time . . ."

"Central China? Then you were there in the early stage of the war?"

"Sure, just after it broke out. I went there in August. First, Shanghai, then to Changshu, Wusieh. . . ."

"Nanking?"

"Yeah, Nanking. I climbed up that front wall . . . must have been twenty feet, high . . . straight up."

"No, higher than that?"

"You know Nanking, Iwamoto-san?"

"Sure, been there many times. You see, I was an interpreter. I'm pretty good at Chinese," Wu said.

"Really?"

"True. It was terrible, Nanking. We killed a lot. Fifty or sixty thousand. . . ."

"Ah, far more than that. We just couldn't figure out how to dispose of all those corpses. I myself must have got ten, maybe fifteen," Haneda confessed.

"Yeah? Even I got five or six," Wu said, pouring sake into Haneda's glass. "You been near the Military Academy?"

"Sure. That building was turned into a headquarters—later."

"Back of that building, there was a hill commanding a good view, remember?"

"The big mansions, I remember, I remember. Our unit cleared that area."

"There was some people left behind, I think."

"Just old men and women. They begged and begged—mercy—it was really funny."

"Get any loot?"

"Sure, loads. We couldn't carry it around, though we could take anything. We threw it all away. And then, anyway, I was sent back wounded around then."

"Then you didn't bring back anything?"

"Nothing—except a little watch I took—"

"A watch? That'd be a good souvenir. Where'd you get it?"

"Let me see—an old woman. She had a good watch . . . from an old woman. I tried to take it . . . She wouldn't let me have it. Then an old man told her to let it go. He spoke some Japanese . . ."

"Yes . . . and then you . . ."

"I guess so . . . anyway, they're dead. We were busy mopping up, you see, so I locked 'em up in a room and threw in a hand-grenade . . . I went away, busy . . . I don't know what happened . . . besides, who cares? Just some old Chinese . . ." Haneda was so tight that he probably didn't even remember his words the next day.

Wu finally knew the murderer of his parents. Yet that night he slept in the same room with Haneda, as if nothing had happened.

Mr. Wu Kao-chih, however, began scheming to kill Haneda. Yumiko tried to persuade him to hold his hand, but Wu did not listen. He cold-bloodedly checked every possibility of murdering Haneda—or in his words, avenging his parents. Take him mountain climbing and push him off a cliff; drugs; fake auto-accident; push him from an express train. Every possible murder-method Wu thought over and re-checked, and rejected. On the other hand, he kept Haneda in a good mood, still supplying him with goods at cheap prices.

Then, a tragedy took place. On October 3, 1950, Yachiyo, the daughter of Yumiko, mysteriously disappeared on her way home from school. That evening Yumiko reported her daughter presumably kidnapped to the police and a search was begun.

The police went to Haneda's house only to find no trace of the girl. Haneda set up a firm alibi and was instantly cleared. Three days passed without news of the missing girl.

Yumiko lost her composure. Mr. Wu seemed to have been of help, at least in public, as her friends report. But he did not try to deal directly with Haneda. "Mr. Wu Kao-chih, protector of the missing girl," knew such action would spoil his hopes of revenge. Yumiko was no longer normal—sleepless nights, days of worry. On the third night, when Mr. Wu was away, she dashed out of the house. How she got there she could not remember, but later that night she was standing in front of Haneda's house in Ueno.

She knocked at the door. Haneda came out. She pounced on him, screaming, "Give me back Yachiyo. Give her back!" Haneda called the nearby police box. The police officer came, listened to the trouble, but hesitated to get involved in some family squabble between a man and a woman who had once lived together, someplace else. It was out of his jurisdiction, he claimed, and put Yumiko into a taxi, telling her to go home.

She didn't. She came back to Haneda's again, went inside the garden. She set fire to several places around and under the house. Flames spread; the fire enveloped the whole four-room house.

Neighbors were alarmed. Yumiko was seen crazily jumping around the flaming house, shouting, again and again, "Give me back my Yachiyo." She was caught by the police.

Haneda's wife narrowly escaped. But Haneda himself was found the next morning, a burned body among the ashes and rubble.

In the afternoon an employee of Haneda's shop came to the Ueno police station to give himself up, bringing Yachiyo with him. He had been ordered by Haneda to kidnap the girl and take her to Odawara. Hiding there for several days, he had read of the tragedy in the newspaper.

In February, 1951, Yumiko Ueda was sentenced to serve five years in Toyotama Penitentiary. Mr. Wu arranged to send Yachiyo to Yumiko's brother in the country.

In May, 1951, Mr. Wu Kao-chih disposed of all his business affairs and his properties. In June, he left Japan. A few days before taking a CAT plane for Hongkong he paid a visit to Yumiko in the Penitentiary. "I guess, I owe you so much," he said. "You did the thing in my behalf. Because of you, I did not become a murderer. Yet my parents have been avenged."

He handed her a one-million-yen time-deposit certificate and an ivory signature seal with which to claim it, and said, "I am leaving Japan for good. When you are released, please use this money for yourself and Yachiyo-san. I'll be wishing for your happiness, from a faraway land."

Then he left.

In February, 1953, her lawyer arranged her release on bond using part of the money Mr. Wu had left. Yumiko went back to her brother's where Yachiyo was staying. In August of that year, a beautiful London-made jewelry box was delivered from Mr. Wu. There was no sender's address, just the postmark "Nanking." No further news has come from Mr. Wu, since then. But Yumiko Ueda is living peacefully, helping out on her brother's farm.

In that jewelry box lies the seal Mr. Wu had specially made for Yumiko—an ivory seal, with the arabesque design of a little red flower inlaid in the top.

*Haruto Ko (b. 1906), a novelist of considerable talent, is little known outside Japan. Early in his career, he wrote poetry with a humanistic tone, but he later turned to the novel. His simple, direct style, somewhat reminiscent of Hemingway, and the absence of any attempt to preach make him unusual among Japanese writers. Critics have praised his fiction for its quiet humor and unique poetic quality.*

*Mistakenly accused of being a Communist, Ko suffered police persecution during World World II. He spent the immediate postwar years in extreme poverty. Most of his writing is autobiographical, reflecting his experiences during the war and its aftermath. One of his novels that is not about his life is* Lost Fatherland *(1959). It deals with a spy case involving a German named Sorge who was arrested by the Japanese in 1941 on suspicion of spying for the Soviet Union.*

*"Black Market Blues," set in the difficult period following World War II, is Ko's only work to be translated into English.*

# Black Market Blues

## by HARUTO KO

TRANSLATED BY GRACE SUZUKI AND JAY GLUCK

Ohizumi met Jack Kurosawa in front of Shimbashi Station and the two walked toward Tamura-cho. The streets were full of Christmas decorations; there were many show windows that had big and small Santas. It was only three days until Christmas.

"Don't worry. I've heard that there's never been a miss so far," Jack assured Ohizumi, looking at him from under his hunting cap.

"I don't know anything about this fellow Buchanan we are about to see," Ohizumi said bluntly. "I put my trust in you, you know that."

Ohizumi had never had any previous dealings with Buchanan. He had not wanted to come to Tokyo with the dangerous dollars in

115

his pocket. His wife Takako did not want him to, either. Ohizumi did all his buying and selling of dollars at his hideout in Kamakura. Those who wanted to sell or buy came to him, and he did his business sitting down, but these last few days he was rushed with dollars. He'd got rid of most of them, but the five thousand he had taken yesterday gave him a big headache. He could not refuse the money because of some obligations from the past. He felt, when he bought the money, that he would have a hard time with it. Sure enough, he could not get rid of it in one day. It was too close to Christmas, and though everyone wanted dollars, no one had enough yen for them.

"It's such a big amount, you know," Jack said, keeping his voice down. "Buchanan is about the only person who can buy such an amount so close to Christmas." Ohizumi felt that Jack was trying to make him feel obligated to him, which annoyed him. He intended to give Jack about fifty thousand commission if the deal went through. He knew, of course, that after Christmas there would be no sale of dollars. He nodded to Jack, looking sharply right and left from behind the gold-rimmed glasses that he used for disguise. Outwardly his easy manner and big shoulders made him look like a boxer, but he was constantly conscious of the five thousand dollars in his pocket.

"I know it's the way with this business. When it comes in like this, I have a hard time getting rid of it," Ohizumi had to confess. "I've got to find more new outlets."

Ohizumi intended making this his last deal. After Christmas, through New Year's, he intended to take Takako to Osaka and hide there for a while. Jack didn't know this, so he answered him light-heartedly. "After we get there, if you feel it isn't safe, we can always leave without doing any business," he said. "There is the Radio Japan Building. It's not so far now."

Ohizumi could hardly hear Jack for the noise on the street. Ohizumi intended doing just that, leaving the office if he smelled anything. The money was not all his; a part of it belonged to Moriwaki, his partner in this business.

They turned the corner and entered a street that was like the bottom of a gorge, then stopped in front of a six-story building with granite stone steps. They walked up to the third floor—they did not use the elevator—and knocked on a door. Beside the door hung a small wooden plaque with Buchanan's name in Japanese. Ohizumi did not fail to note the position of the elevator before he reached that door.

Inside, they were shown to some chairs by a tall blonde who disappeared into the next room. "Let's sit down," Jack said and buried himself in a big chair.

Ohizumi followed suit, and asked, "What kind of a fellow is this Buchanan?" He said it as if wondering about it himself, and not as a question. "What does he do?" This was more like a question.

"I really don't know," Jack said.

Ohizumi had asked the same thing before on the way here and got the same answer. At that time Ohizumi had thought Jack wanted to keep his client's business a secret—not say too much about him—but Ohizumi understood now that Jack really did not know. He made sure of the two exits—one that they had just used and the other through which the blonde had disappeared.

There are those who run away after getting the money, and those who point a gun, he thought. "Did you do your business in this room, too?" he asked Jack.

"Yes, I waited a long time then, too," Jack answered. "Not even a cup of tea. I don't even remember what Buchanan looks like. Come to think of it, I don't even know that it was him," he muttered between puffs of his cigarette.

The fact that Buchanan was willing to buy five thousand dollars told Ohizumi that he was not just an ordinary black market dollar dealer. Ohizumi looked at his watch. It was past three. If he was robbed of this money, he would be finished. He had never been robbed before, but he knew of many who had. One of them committed suicide. It was a distasteful business, but the takes were big. Even after dividing the share with Moriwaki, there should be one thousand yen in it for him.

Twenty minutes passed. He'd finished three cigarettes. "He makes us wait, doesn't he?" Ohizumi said quietly, but he was restless inside.

"What do you want to do?" Jack asked. Ohizumi knew he couldn't say much; they might be listening in the next room.

Ohizumi looked at his watch again. Thirty minutes had passed, but still no Buchanan. To Ohizumi, Buchanan was "first time," but to Buchanan too, Ohizumi was "first time." There was no reason for him not suspecting that Ohizumi might be a cop. Ohizumi was beginning to feel a choking sensation. "It's bad business, this black market." He tried to think of Takako to calm his nerves.

He'd met Takako in one of the new cabarets. The mouth that dimpled when she smiled was terribly sexy. He had divorced his former wife who had two children by him because she would not come in with him on his black market dealings. Takako told him to quit as soon as he made enough money to start a bar. Most of what he'd made in the past was spent in divorcing his first wife, in marrying Takako, and in buying his hideout in Kamakura. He'd had to start all over again at the beginning of this year—but now, at the end of the year, he had made just about enough to start a bar. I'll quit this time for sure, he thought.

Wonder what she is doing now. She didn't want me to come to Tokyo today. I didn't either, for that matter. Ohizumi was thinking these things when the door to the next room suddenly opened. Ohizumi got up and took a few steps backward, his eyes glued to the big man that walked in with a package under his arm. From past experience Ohizumi felt that it was going to be all right, but it was best to be on guard.

"Did you bring the stuff?" Buchanan asked in broken Japanese, looking at Jack searchingly.

"This fellow has it," Jack answered. He had also gotten to his feet. "This is the one I told you about over the telephone a while ago."

Buchanan shifted his searching gaze from Jack to Ohizumi.

"I have it here," Ohizumi patted his breast pocket. Buchanan put the package on the table. Ohizumi saw at once that it was in thousand-yen notes, for the package, two million yen, would be about one foot four inches square. As these calculations flashed through his mind, Ohizumi's nimble hand unbuttoned his coat and brought out the envelope containing the dollars. Jack stood watching.

Ohizumi put the dollars on the table. It was a breath-taking moment. Their glances imparted fire. Ohizumi did not think anything. He only followed the other's motions. Everything, even his life, depended on this moment, but he did not even think of that.

The deal was over. Ohizumi divided the thousand-yen notes into two, put one into the envelope, and the other into his grip.

Buchanan did not say anything unnecessary. Ohizumi wondered if Buchanan was a German. He did not seem like an American, nor Australian. He imparted a heavy feeling. Ohizumi walked to the door, thinking, Best not to show my back to him.

After getting out of the building, he hurried to the station. He felt the fears that he had not been aware of when he exchanged the money with Buchanan. It's best to return to Kamakura as quickly as possible, he thought. This is the last deal in dollars, the last business of the year for me.

He felt elated when he entered the second-class car of the Yokosuka line. But when he reached home a foreigner was waiting for him. He had brought eight thousand dollars. Ohizumi took it against his better judgment. Maybe it was because the deal with Buchanan had gone off so smoothly, maybe because he had been at the business for years.

Takako was furious. "You said yesterday with that five thousand dollars that you were through."

Ohizumi could not answer back. He felt the error too keenly himself. "It was your fault, Nancy," he answered, using his pet name for her. "You should have sent him back and not let him wait for me."

"All the money we saved to open a bar," she said in tears. "The day after tomorrow is Christmas Eve. Tomorrow I wanted to go shopping with you on the Ginza."

He had invested more than two million yen in this deal. He remembered Jack's advice. But the price had been so cheap. If successful, the profit would be terrific.

"I'll get rid of it tomorrow. Think, we'll net five hundred thousand. We need all the money we can get to start a bar, you know that."

"I know, yes," Takako answered but not cheerfully. "I know the more, the better. But I'm worried."

"Don't worry, I'll get rid of it," he said, trying his best to make Takako feel at ease. "We'll clean up everything the day after tomorrow, celebrate the Eve in Ginza, and leave for Osaka. We'll start the preparations for the bar after we come back, if the coast is clear."

Next day, Ohizumi sat alone in his living room, thinking. The night before he had succeeded in making Takako believe that everything would be all right, but he himself did not really know where to turn to get rid of the eight thousand dollars. He couldn't ask Jack any more. He thought of his co-worker in Yokosuka, but knew he could not handle such a big amount. Then he remembered Peter Nemuro, a boxer by profession. Peter had once traded dollars, but although quick with his fists, he had not been so with his brain; he had suffered one big loss after another and finally quit. He might know of someone. Ohizumi called him in Tokyo by phone. Peter, after hearing that Ohizumi could not talk over the phone, agreed to come to Kamakura immediately.

When Peter came, and listened to Ohizumi, he advised him to go to Jack. Ohizumi told him in detail about his deal with Buchanan. "I think Jack was right. There's only two days to Christmas, you know," he said, and folded his arms.

Then he thought of Fukumoto, who was once a member of the boxing club Peter belonged to.

"Can you contact him right away?" Ohizumi asked quickly, and added, "Can't lose any time, you know."

Peter left after promising to contact Fukumoto immediately. Ohizumi gave him five thousand yen and assurance that there would be more after the deal went through.

The arrangement was made that day for Ohizumi to meet Fukumoto at a tea shop called the Milano off the Ginza. Ohizumi's identification was a brown overcoat and gold-rimmed glasses and Fukumoto, he was told, was a small, pale-faced fellow.

Ohizumi called Moriwaki, his partner, and told him he would call on him about noon the next day, and told him to wait for him. Moriwaki had invested five hundred thousand, and after the deal was over Ohizumi intended to clear the account with him, and wash his hands of the whole nasty business.

When Ohizumi went to the Milano the next day, a small, pale-faced fellow got up from the corner booth. Ohizumi walked up to him.

"Glad to meet you," said the pale-faced fellow and smiled. He was well-mannered, which gave Ohizumi the feeling he was not quite dependable. Then to his mind came the face of Takako who had said with a dark expression just before he left, "I have a bad feeling this morning. Somehow, I don't want you to go today."

He shook off his sense of foreboding and immediately started to talk business. "Is it you who wants to trade?" he asked.

"No, it's not me," Fukumoto answered quickly. "As soon as Peter called me last night, I contacted several and came across a fellow named Seki who said he would buy."

"I see. Where is this fellow Seki?"

"I contacted him just before I came here," Fukumoto continued. "Made arrangements for you to make a deal at a place called Kagetsu in Tsukiji."

Ohizumi wondered why Fukumoto would not take him to Seki's house. He also wondered why he had to wait until three that afternoon. He would have to call Moriwaki and extend the hour of appointment with him.

"It's big money, you know," Fukumoto said. At present market prices what Ohizumi had was equivalent to three million yen. "I suppose Seki has to get the money ready."

"All right then," Ohizumi said. "I'll meet you there with Seki at three. You sure he'll be there?"

"Oh, sure," Fukumoto said.

From there he went to Moriwaki and told him to accompany him to Tsukiji that afternoon. Moriwaki was skeptical about the way

Ohizumi did his business, and said for him to divide his money. Ohizumi replied he did not have time, that he had to get rid of it before Christmas. And all the time he was talking to Moriwaki, he was thinking of Takako, and the prospective bar he was going to operate with her. With her looks it was a cinch men would flock to her bar like bees to flowers. What made him think so much about his new bar was probably his appointment in Tsukiji. About three years earlier at the height of his business he had frequented a place called Kiki-no-ya, the House of Chrysanthemum, in the red light district. He had become chummy with a geisha called Kikuharu, Spring Chrysanthemum. That was before he met Takako. Fond memories of those days came back to him and he only half-heard what Moriwaki was trying to say to him. "Well then, let's meet this fellow Seki," Moriwaki said in the end. "If anything smells bad, all we have to say is we didn't bring the money. Where are we meeting him?"

"That's the funny thing. It's close to Kiku-no-ya."

"Really?" Moriwaki was also amused. "That's very interesting." Moriwaki and Ohizumi both laughed knowingly.

After a quick lunch they left Moriwaki's apartment early. They went straight to Tsukiji to have a look at the place first. Moriwaki carried the money, for they thought it best that Ohizumi should go there alone without anything on him. They first went to a small tea shop where there was a phone. Ohizumi took down the phone number and told Moriwaki to come to Kagetsu as soon as he called.

Ohizumi then went to Kagetsu. The house had a black fence on the street side, which shut out the street noise. Once inside, Ohizumi had the illusion that he had come far, far away from the Ginza. The girl who met him at the entrance hall took him to a room with an expensive-looking *tokonoma*, with all its usual hanging scrolls, flower arrangement and art objects. She asked him to wait. She sat on the *tatami* at the exit, her finger tips touching the *tatami* as she bowed, got up, slipped out, got down on her knees again to close the sliding partition. Her quiet graceful manners, typical of *machiai* or tea house and high-class Japanese restaurant waitresses, reminded him again of the time he used to come to these places often. Then he was dealing in cigarettes and food stuffs, sending out his assistants with two or three truck loads every day. His biggest clients were these *machiai* places and high-class restaurants.

While Ohizumi sat thinking of these things, the partition opened and Fukumoto came in. "Seki was waiting for you, but he said you might be late and he went to the theater," he explained as he sat down. Ohizumi thought it odd. He knew he was not very late. He thought afterward that this was when he should have smelled something, when he should have quit the place.

"Did you bring the money with you this time?" Fukumoto asked.

"I don't have it with me now," Ohizumi said. "But my partner has it—he's waiting for my call in a nearby tea shop."

"Well then, please call him," Fukumoto said getting to his feet again. "I'll send for Seki at the theater." He left the room.

Ohizumi called Moriwaki, and told him to come. In the meantime, the waitress carried in cakes and fruit and put them on the table. Moriwaki came immediately, and Fukumoto joined them, saying Seki would come right away. Ohizumi thought it odd again; for he knew that though it takes a little time to call a person out from a theater, this was taking a little too long. Just then the partition at Ohizumi's back opened wide, and three big foreigners came in. Ohizumi and the others jumped to their feet. One of the three foreigners, a red-faced giant of a fellow, pointed a gun at them.

"We're C.I.D.s," he barked. "Put up your hands."

Ohizumi was quiet. He slowly put his hands up, and scrutinized Fukumoto sharply. Fukumoto was pale. Ohizumi wondered if this was Fukumoto's doing.

"Why are you carrying dollars?" the red face continued. "We're going to question you."

Ohizumi thought then that they were fakes. The investigations were always carried out at headquarters, not at a place like this. He thought of all these things while watching one of the three men search Moriwaki, and take out the eight thousand dollars he had in his pocket. He gritted his teeth— Ohizumi would not have let him have it that easy; he would have jumped out of the window before he let these fakes have it.

"It's our business if we carry dollars," Ohizumi yelled. "We carry any amount for our business. If you want to investigate, take us to your headquarters."

"We'll take you to headquarters," the big fellow said, with a mocking smile. "Walk," he said, and pointed the gun at the three Japanese.

Seki did not show up till the end.

After they were shoved into a car, the three foreigners stopped another taxi. This fact assured Ohizumi that they were fakes; if they had been C.I.D.s, they would have been there with a jeep. Inside, alone in the car, Ohizumi put his big hands around Fukumoto's neck. "How dare you fool us like this?" Ohizumi said between his teeth.

"I don't know, I don't know anything," Fukumoto wailed and cried like a baby.

"Then it's Seki, Fukumoto was only a decoy," Ohizumi decided.

The car with the three foreigners was following their car, but the distance between the two got greater and greater, and finally it disappeared.

"Turn the car back to Kagetsu," Ohizumi ordered. But the people at Kagetsu did not know Seki, said he had never been there before.

Ohizumi turned again to Fukumoto, but he only sobbed, "I only did it so I might make some extra money for the New Year."

Fukumoto knew the apartment where Seki lived, but when they went there Seki had already moved out. They learned then that Seki was a Chinese by the name of Sai. Ohizumi, for the first time, ate dirt—and hard.

Just as he came out of the Ikuta Building, Ohizumi was stopped by a policeman.

"I want to ask you something," he said. Ohizumi did his best to suppress his fear and remain calm. Could Fukumoto, whom he had just left, have reported him? It couldn't be.

"What do you want," Ohizumi said slowly.

"Not here," said the policeman, "Please come to headquarters." The policeman was extremely polite, with a faint smile flickering around his mouth all the time. Ohizumi was glad he did not have any dollars on him. In his pocket were a few yen notes, and an I.O.U. he'd just had Fukumoto write out for the money he'd been robbed of by the fake C.I.D.s. He wanted to report the robbery but to do that was to chance being arrested himself.

"I am not doing anything," he said, his eyes darting sharply right and left, remembering to keep a smile. "I don't know what you want, but ask me here, if you want."

"It won't take long," said the young policeman, still polite. "I only want you to come with me for a little while."

The policeman was asking him, not ordering him. Perhaps it is nothing to worry about, Ohizumi told himself. Because of his past job during the war—he was once a private secretary of a minister— he had many friends everywhere. If anything went wrong, he could ask their help, though he wasn't quite sure about getting it.

"If you are not going to tell me why, I don't have to go," Ohizumi said firmly. "I am busy. Besides if you want to arrest me, you'll have to take the proper procedure."

The policeman seemed to think it best not to rile him. He said gently, "Were you not robbed of some dollars by some fake C.I.D.s?"

So that's it, it was Fukumoto. He reported because he couldn't pay. The reason he was robbed was because Fukumoto was a fool and was now trying to get him this way— I'll kill him! He mulled these things over in his mind quickly.

"Don't know anything about fake C.I.D.s," he barked. "I'm busy, don't you see? I can't be bothered. I live in Kamakura, and come to Tokyo only to do business."

"We know you live in Kamakura," the policeman said. "Do you come to Tokyo every day these days?" The policeman's manner remained calm and polite. Cold sweat came over Ohizumi; so they were following him. "There were others who were robbed besides you," the policeman continued, unmindful of Ohizumi's fear. "One of them reported and the fake C.I.D.s were picked up. They confessed everything. We checked with the *machiai* house in Tsukiji about you."

Ohizumi thought for a moment to give up to the police, and then changed his mind quickly. What's wrong with me these days? he thought. If I complain, I'm only confirming that I traded in dollars.

Conversation dragged on for a while but in the end the policeman gave up, and said, "I'll report to my chief that you would not come. That's all I can do for now," and they parted.

Clad in a dull, yolk-colored overcoat of English material, Ohizumi looked the prosperous businessman, but since the fake C.I.D. incident, his money was all gone, and he was having a hard time figuring out how he was going to pay his bills. He walked into the Lilac tea shop, where he had once carried out million-yen deals.

"Has Akiyama been here?" he asked the head waiter.

"No," he answered without changing expression, and whispered something to a waitress.

She came up to Ohizumi and said in a low voice, "Mr. Akiyama called and said he would be here about four," and left to fill his order.

"Wonder what he wants." Ohizumi looked at his watch. Forty minutes more until four. He drank his coffee, and left the tea shop to kill time, leaving word that he would be back.

When he got back, Akiyama was waiting for him. "I've news for you," Akiyama said as soon as he saw Ohizumi. Akiyama was excited. "Kamioka is here in Tokyo. He's driving a big car. One of the only three such cars in Japan now, the latest model Chrysler."

Kamioka was in the textile black market, but Ohizumi had loaned him money a couple of times before. "He went to Kobe, didn't he?" Ohizumi asked. "I think of him once in a while. He was a quiet fellow," he added.

"Said he wanted to see you," Akiyama went on. "He will be here at two tomorrow. I thought sure he was having a hard time," said Akiyama.

"Yeah, he was kind of slow, as I remember him," Ohizumi said. "Is he an auto broker?"

"No, I think he's in this," and Akiyama made a gesture of giving a shot to his knee.

"Maybe I'll borrow some money from him," Ohizumi said, thinking back to the days when he was able to lend one or two million yen to his friends easily. Now his position had been reversed.

"Kamioka wants me to go to Kobe with him, and I think I will." Akiyama said. "He said he'd find me clients. I've got to deal with foreigners in my line of business. Why don't you go, too?"

"If I were young like you—" Ohizumi said. He didn't know what Takako would say.

Akiyama smiled at that. Ohizumi, who once couldn't be without a woman one night, had stopped going to bars and cabarets after he had married Takako. After the baby, Tamako, was born, he went home early every night.

Ohizumi met Kamioka at the Lilac the next day. He looked quite dapper in his gray overcoat and soft hat. When he had gone home the night before, he'd told Takako about being stopped by the police and about Kamioka, and told her that he might borrow some money from him. Takako was pleased, and they both forgot about the nasty business of the police, talking for hours about opening the bar.

"Let's go out," Kamioka said, after the greetings were over. "I've got my car outside."

The car they got into passed the front of the Piccadilly Theater and crossed the bridge. Kamioka came close to Ohizumi, and said low, "Heard about your mishap at Tsukiji. It was a darn shame."

"Yeah, a rotten business," Ohizumi said. "The place made me a bit careless. And I got stopped by police yesterday, too. One bad thing after another. I want to quit this business and start a bar with my wife," he said in the end. "I want to help your work a few days, to make enough to start this bar."

Kamioka put his hand into his pocket and drew out a newspaper bundle. "Please use this," he said. "I have lots of money now."

"I will borrow it then," Ohizumi said. He felt the money from outside, and thought it contained about a million yen. "I am going to use this money to help you, and make some capital for the bar. I have a hunch the police are after me, so I don't want to take too many chances, and also, I want to quit it in two or three days."

"Okay," Kamioka said cheerfully. "I'll make the contacts for you right away. My name's George Mizuki, remember."

Their business was risky. They made a lot at a time, but they lost big, too. Once Ohizumi was followed by the police and he had to throw into a gutter drugs worth five hundred thousand yen. At one time a loss of three million yen meant nothing to him. Now everything was different. It had become hard work to make fifty thousand.

When he went home, Takako met him with a letter from the policeman he'd met that day in Tokyo. It said that the police would not inconvenience him in any way, and therefore wished him to come to police headquarters.

In the course of the following few days, he was followed constantly by the police. In three days he made enough money to start the bar and was busy getting things in shape.

One day after he had been to see Fukumoto to get the money the latter was paying him bit by bit, he was walking toward the Lilac to meet Sedo, his new partner in the bar business whom Akiyama had introduced him to. He was told that Sedo's wife had worked in a bar, and that Sedo was once a manager in a hotel in Atami. He neared Sukiyabashi Bridge, and turned back, from sheer habit, only to see the same old policeman. Cold sweat came over him.

"You did not come after all," the policeman said, smiling. "We waited for you."

"But don't you see," Ohizumi had calmed by this time, "as I told you the last time, I had nothing to do with it."

"There are Japanese, Koreans, and Chinese who were robbed just like you," the young policeman said quietly. "The total money stolen was fifteen million yen. The fake C.I.D. men were caught, but we need witnesses to confirm the crime. I'll see that no harm will come to you. Please come with me."

"But I am busy," Ohizumi answered bluntly.

"I know that, but the American court requires witnesses." The policeman was half pleading. "Those who were robbed all say the same thing you do."

"If you make it so that I was robbed of yen," Ohizumi said, "then I'll come with you."

"That's all right," the policeman was quick to agree. "All you have to say is that you were robbed by the men in Tsukiji."

"If you fool me, I'll never forgive you," Ohizumi threatened.

"Sure thing," the policeman assured. "I won't cause you any trouble."

Ohizumi got into a taxi with him. When they arrived at headquarters and saw the officer in charge, Ohizumi was told the man who reported the robbery was a Japanese, a former Navy Officer. He was robbed of eight hundred dollars, but when the fake C.I.D.s got in the jeep, he took the number and reported. They arrested a C.I.D. First Lieutenant, by the name of Burton, and another C.I.D. Sergeant by the name of Michael.

"Burton has confessed," the officer told Ohizumi. "They asked us to investigate, and your name came up."

"I thought it was kind of funny," Ohizumi admitted. "But I could do nothing at the point of a gun."

"They are going to have a trial next Thursday," the officer continued, "And they want you to appear as a witness."

"I am busy with my business," Ohizumi told the officer.

"We know that, but according to the American procedures they cannot establish a crime unless supported by witnesses," the officer explained. "We had about three appearing, but they all backed down at the crucial time. We want you to please have courage and be a witness."

The officer pleaded with him. Ohizumi thought of Takako and the newborn baby. After all, the dollars robbed from him would not return, and he did not want any part in a trial. But at the same time he did not want to be labeled a coward. The police had been following him for the last few days, and must know of his activities in dope peddling. It might be wiser to listen to their wish now.

"The policeman who brought me here said you would fix it so

that I was robbed of yen and not dollars," Ohizumi said. "I'll be the witness with that agreement."

"Yes, that's all right. We'll do that," the officer said, an expression of relief coming over him.

"I have my wife and a baby to think of, you know," Ohizumi said. "I don't want to be pinched, on top of being robbed."

"I don't blame you a bit," the officer said, smiling. "The court martial will be held not very far from here. You can go see the officer of the judicial affairs across the street from there and work it out with him."

Ohizumi knew that it was bad to deal in black market dollars. But it was not only men like him who dealt in them. There were many politicians who bought dollars in large amounts. If the military law officer would agree to Ohizumi's proposition, he had decided to be their witness, to prevent more Japanese being robbed by men like Burton and Michael.

He spent the rest of the day on the business of his new bar. He doubled the money he borrowed from Kamioka in three days and returned the million he had borrowed. For the new bar, Sedo would put in two million yen, just twice Ohizumi's amount. The profit would be divided into four and six. Ohizumi also agreed to register the bar under Sedo's wife's name, in order to be prepared for any unforeseen outcome of the military trial.

The next day he went to see the judiciary officer to get his agreement.

On the day of the trial he went to the place as directed. He got off the elevator on the fourth floor, and started to walk down the hall. He met a huge man—a face he had not forgotten. Seeing Ohizumi, the man growled at him in broken Japanese. "If you testify, I'll do this to you," and he drew his open hand across his throat. "You'll be sent to Okinawa, maybe."

According to American law, until a crime is established against a person, that man can go about as a free man. No wonder no one was willing to testify.

Ohizumi only smiled. He had given up the dollar black market. He'd already got the money to start his bar. He had returned the money to Kamioka, too. If anything should happen to him, Takako and his baby could live on the profit from the bar.

He entered the waiting room. There were two Chinese, a man and a woman, both young. They had dark expressions on their faces. Burton came in, this time with another tall fellow Ohizumi remembered. This must be Michael. They both threatened in their broken Japanese, while an MP looked on expressionless.

The time came and they entered the court room. When he sat down in the witness chair, he forgot about Takako and his baby. He forgot about the new bar he was about to open. He only remembered the mortifying feeling he went through when he was robbed by the two men he was about to testify against.

"These are the men," he yelled. "These are the men who robbed me of three million yen," he said, renewing the fear and remorse he felt when the money was taken from him.

About a month later, he heard Burton and Michael had been sent back to their country. He was paid for the four days he spent testifying at the court.

His new bar was opened near Kyobashi. It was christened the Pearl, but Sedo and his wife would not give him his share of the profit. It was registered under Sedo's wife's name, so there was nothing Ohizumi could do about it.

Ohizumi gave it all up. He just wasn't cut out for the rackets. There was an honest job open in a lumber company and he made an appointment with the personnel director.

*Seicho Matsumoto (b. 1909) has been acclaimed as Japan's number one mystery writer since 1957 when his novel* Points and Lines *became a blockbuster success. Of humble origin, without a university education, he has risen to the top of the writing profession. His books are on the best-seller lists year after year. Besides crime fiction, he also writes historical novels and essays on such subjects as archeology and the Japanese economy. A prolific author, Matsumoto has found time in recent years to become involved in motion picture production. He has his own film company, Kiri Productions, and supervises the making of movies based on his novels.*

*Perhaps as important as the books Matsumoto writes is his leadership of the "social detective" school of mystery fiction. He urges fellow writers to strive for realism and to stress motivation. Summing up his approach to crime writing, he said, "I include all the essential strains of mystery, but cannot omit surroundings and circumstances. I cannot help but write about present conditions and the way people live."*

*Only one novel by Matsumoto,* Points and Lines *(trans. 1970), is available in English. One of his short stories can be found in* Ellery Queen's Japanese Golden Dozen *(1978); three have appeared in* Ellery Queen's Mystery Magazine; *and one is in* Ellery Queen's Prime Crimes *(1983).*

# The Secret Alibi

## by SEICHO MATSUMOTO

Chieko Umetani was sitting in front of the mirror putting on her makeup. The small dressing table had been bought for her the previous month by Teiichiro Ishino—in fact, he had bought all the furniture in the room. The apartment was small—it consisted of only two rooms, each about nine feet by nine; but Chieko had managed to furnish it in such a way as to create the impression of space.

It was obviously the apartment of a young person and it was painted in a warm color that always made forty-eight-year-old Ishino feel refreshed when he came there. His own house was much larger and more luxurious, but it was cold and colorless. Even when

133

he was at home with his family, he found the lack of warm color depressing, and when he opened his eyes in the morning he felt as if all his own warmth was being sucked out of him.

Ishino changed quickly into his clothes, and lying on the floor with his head propped up with one hand, he lit a cigarette. As he lay there watching the girl in the mirror, he was struck by her youth. The clothes she wore, the way she put on her makeup, her voice—everything about her was young and fresh, a far cry from the wife who was waiting for him at home.

Chieko was in her early twenties and had worked in the same department as Ishino until about two months before. Ishino was proud of his position as a department head in the company, and not wanting to endanger his future with rumors of an illicit affair, he had persuaded Chieko to leave work soon after they had got together, and had rented this apartment for her.

Ishino lived in southern Tokyo, and when he looked for the apartment, he chose a place where no one else from the office would be likely to bump into him. He eventually found this apartment in Nishi-Okubo, to the west of Tokyo, and for his clandestine purpose it was perfect. Not only was it out of the way, but it was situated at the junction of two narrow alleyways and he could always slip in and out without being seen. Chieko had rented the rooms in her own name, and as he never visited her during the day he felt there was no chance he would be connected with her in any way. Chieko thought it all very amusing and told him that no one in the neighborhood so much as suspected his existence. Although the houses in Tokyo are all crowded together, the people who live in them are isolated from each other.

"I'm sorry I took so long," Chieko said. She got up and turned to Ishino with a smile. "And what excuse are you going to give your good wife this evening?"

Ishino took his hand from behind his head and looked at his watch. "It's only nine o'clock. I'll tell her I went to a film at Shibuya—the timing is just about right."

He stood up and helped Chieko on with her coat.

"But what if she asks you about the plot of the movie?"

"The film I saw last week is still running. I'll tell her about that."

They looked at each other and started to laugh.

Chieko left the house first, and going out to the street she checked that there was no one around before giving Ishino the all-clear signal. Despite his precautions Ishino was always afraid they might be seen together, but Chieko was insistent that she at least see him to a taxi. He insisted, however, that she walk a few paces behind him, and when he hailed a taxi that she wait a short distance away in a darkened entrance. In this way, even if they happened to be seen by someone, there was nothing to connect them with each other.

The night of December the 14th was still quite warm when Ishino walked ahead of Chieko toward the busy main road about 200 yards away. He had only about 50 feet to go when suddenly a man walking in the opposite direction recognized him and bowed. Ishino panicked slightly, but as the man walked under a street light, Ishino recognized him as Kozo Sugiyama, a neighbor from Omori whom he knew only by sight. Without thinking, Ishino bowed, and instantly regretted it.

Why did I do that? he thought. I had only to ignore him and he would probably think he'd made a mistake. After all, it's night time and he wouldn't be expecting to see me here. I wonder what he was doing here at this time of night. He looks like an office worker but—oh, how annoying.

He walked into the main road and was waiting for a taxi to appear when Chieko moved up beside him and asked in a low voice, "Did you know that man?"

She had seen their exchange of bows.

"Yes, it was one of my neighbors."

"Oh . . ." Chieko murmured. "Is it all right?"

She sounded quite worried.

"I think so."

"He won't tell your wife, will he?"

"No, we aren't really on speaking terms—we just know each other by sight."

Chieko was silent for a few moments. There was still no sign of a taxi, and Ishino was just thinking of asking Chieko to stand away from him when she said anxiously, "Do you think he guessed . . . about us?"

Ishino was startled.

"If he suspected something he might talk about it and rumors might get back to your wife."

"You were walking behind me, weren't you?"

"Yes."

"Did he look at you when he passed?"

"No, he walked straight past."

"Then there's nothing to worry about—he didn't suspect anything," said Ishino in a relieved voice.

"You're sure?"

"Yes, don't worry. But move away a bit, will you?"

Chieko walked off, her heels ringing on the pavement just as an empty taxi came down the street.

Sitting in the swaying taxi, Ishino thought back over everything Chieko had said.

"I wonder if Sugiyama will mention having seen me. If even a hint gets back to my wife, if she hears I was in Okubo with a young woman, she's sure to cause a scene. And if she makes a big enough fuss, they could learn about it at the office and I could get demoted."

Ishino put these thoughts aside, realizing it did no good to worry about them. The taxi was now speeding along the outer loop, and opening the window he let the cold night air rush in to clear his head.

He glanced at his watch as he got out of the cab in front of his home in Omori and saw that it was 9:45. As he approached the front door, the porch light came on and he heard his wife's harsh voice call out in greeting.

Looking at her fat figure, his thoughts went back to Chieko's lithe form, and he felt his usual depression closing in around him.

"You're late," she said as he struggled with the laces of his shoes.

"Yes, I took in a movie at Shibuya on the way home."

Ishino stepped out of his shoes and hurried through to the living room. Glancing around, he couldn't help wondering again why this house always seemed so cold and dreary. His wife came into the room carrying a kimono for him to change into.

"Would you like your dinner now?" she asked.

"No, I've eaten," Ishino answered tersely. His wife looked disgruntled, but didn't say anything more. Seeing that he was going to be left in peace, Ishino relaxed, and after having a cigarette he went to bed.

The next morning he awoke with the sunlight pouring through the thin paper sliding doors. The morning newspaper was lying by his pillow and reaching out, he picked it up and started to look through it. There was a headline:

## YOUNG HOUSEWIFE MURDERED BY ROBBER IN MUKOJIMA

The third page of the newspaper was filled with news of the murder and Teiichiro Ishino gave the story a cursory reading.

"A twenty-three-year-old housewife was attacked and strangled by a burglar while she was alone in her home in the Mukojima area. The body was discovered by her husband when he returned from work . . ."

It was quite a common story these days and Teiichiro didn't bother to read on. He closed his eyes and was just about to drop off to sleep again when he thought of Chieko alone in her apartment every day, and he couldn't help but worry.

During the next two weeks nothing out of the ordinary happened. He visited Chieko only once.

"Did that man we saw last time say anything?" she asked.

"No, it's okay. He obviously didn't notice you, so we have nothing to worry about."

For a moment Kozo Sugiyama's long thin face swam in front of his eyes.

"Now that you mention it, I haven't seen the man since then," he said almost to himself.

"That's good," Chieko said, smiling.

\*   \*   \*

One day, at about three o'clock, Ishino was examining some documents when the office porter came in and told him that he had visitors. Looking at the card, he saw that it belonged to Inspector Tameo Okudaira of the Central Police Department. Teiichiro thought he must have come in some connection with Chieko and his face started to burn.

"There are three of them," the porter added.

Teiichiro asked him to show them into the reception room. In order to appear calm and casual he purposely took his time in going out to meet them. He found, however, that he was so upset that he could make no sense out of what he was reading, and giving it up, he hurried down to the reception room.

There were three men in plainclothes sitting along one side of the oval table. As Ishino entered, all three stood, and Teiichiro noticed that the one on the left was much older than the other two.

"Good afternoon," he said in a calm voice. "I'm Teiichiro Ishino. What can I do for you?"

"Okudaira," said the oldest of the three, bowing politely to Teiichiro.

The Inspector introduced the other two detectives, but Teiichiro immediately forgot their names. Inspector Okudaira had a square face and looked more like a merchant than a policeman. He kept smiling and chatting in a friendly way while the porter brought in the tea. Teiichiro struck a match and lit a cigarette, but not knowing why they had come to see him he couldn't relax.

"To get down to business," said Okudaira, taking out his notebook. "You live at Omori Magome, Ota-ku, don't you?" and he mentioned the street number.

"Yes, that's right," Teiichiro answered in the same calm voice, his heart beating furiously.

The detective stared at him in a most unsettling way.

What's he got written in that notebook? Teiichiro thought.

"We came here to ask you about one of your neighbors, a Mr. Kozo Sugiyama. You know him, don't you?"

Teiichiro was surprised by this turn of events, but bearing in mind their chance meeting weeks ago, he realized that he had to be careful, that he could not let down his guard.

"I know him by sight, but I don't think I have ever spoken to him."

"But you'd recognize him if you met him somewhere?"

"Yes, of course I'd recognize him," Teiichiro said, his meeting Sugiyama at Nishi-Okubo springing into his mind again. —Just what was this detective driving at?

"In that case, I wonder if you remember having passed him in the street at Nishi-Okubo on the evening of December the fourteenth?"

So that's it, thought Teiichiro. It *was* the fourteenth.

Thinking quickly about Chieko, he realized it would be best if he denied any knowledge of having seen Sugiyama.

"Let me see . . ." he said, pretending to be searching his memory.

"What's this all about, anyway?" he asked, trying to get a clue as to what he should say.

"We're investigating a very serious case," the detective answered. "There was a murder at Mukojima at nine o'clock on the night of the fourteenth. You may have read about it in the newspapers—a young housewife was murdered.

"Well, it happens that our main suspect is Mr. Sugiyama. The evidence against him is very strong, but he claims he bumped into you on the street in Nishi-Okubo at the time in question and that if we were to ask you, you would be able to confirm it.

"Nishi-Okubo being a considerable distance from Mukojima, he couldn't possibly have been in both places at the same time and it would give him a perfect alibi. Therefore I want you to think very carefully before you answer, because you are his only witness."

Teiichiro was shocked. He couldn't think of a worse situation in which to have met Sugiyama. If he admitted having seen him, his affair with Chieko was sure to become public and the thought of what that would mean filled him with distress.

"No, I can't say that I ever saw him there," Teiichiro said clearly.

Ishino went straight home after work. He still hadn't recovered from the shock of the police coming to his office, and although he really didn't care about Sugiyama's predicament, he was worried that the police might somehow connect him with Chieko. It was almost as if it was a trap to catch him.

Why was Sugiyama a suspect in the Mukojima murder anyway? Teiichiro had certainly met him at nine o'clock, as Sugiyama had said. Sugiyama had bowed to him and without thinking, he had bowed back. All he had to do was admit this and Sugiyama would be in the clear. But if he did, his own position would be endangered. If anyone found out about Chieko, he would suffer in more ways than one. No, it was unfortunate about Sugiyama, but Teiichiro wasn't about to sacrifice his comfort and his position for another man.

His wife came to the door as he arrived.

"You're home early today," she said.

Teiichiro gave her his briefcase and undid his shoes in silence.

"Have you heard?" she asked in her rasping voice as she followed him into the living room, "About that nice Mr. Sugiyama? They say he murdered that woman at Mukojima! Isn't it terrible?" she asked, her eyes wide with excitement.

Teiichiro wasn't sure what he should say. He remained silent.

"Although we didn't know anything about it, they say he was arrested three days ago. I was very surprised—he looks like such a quiet man. It just goes to show—you can't judge by appearances."

"The police were searching his house today and asking all the neighbors about him. They say his wife was in tears, but it's his three children I feel sorry for, you know?"

His wife was so full of the affair she was much more talkative than usual.

Teiichiro couldn't make up his mind whether to tell her about the detectives coming to his office. He thought it over while he changed, then went to join her in the kitchen. Finally he decided that in a major case like this one the police were sure to be back to check his story and she would find out anyway.

"Actually the police came to see me at the office today about it," he said in a casual manner.

His wife looked at him in amazement.

"Sugiyama claims he saw me in Nishi-Okubo at the time the

murder was committed. I had no reason to be in that area, but he insists he saw me there. I suppose he hopes to save himself with lies."

"What did you tell them?" his wife asked.

"Of course I told them he was lying. I'm not going to commit perjury to save someone I hardly know."

His wife nodded understandingly, then asked, "Where were you at that time?"

Her eyes seemed to flash suspiciously and momentarily he was alarmed.

"I was watching that film at Shibuya. Don't you remember, the time I was late getting home."

"Oh, yes, I remember." She nodded to herself for a few moments, then said angrily, "But why does he have to drag you into it? What has he got against you?"

"He just wants to save himself. Desperate people will say anything if they think it will save them," Teiichiro said calmly, but suddenly he felt cold as he realized that he was the one who was telling a lie to save himself. He was determined, however, that no one would learn the truth no matter how many innocent people he had to sacrifice. He had to look after himself first. Even if Sugiyama had noticed Chieko and told the police about her, he would stick to his story and deny all knowledge of her. If he insisted that he didn't meet anyone after he left the film, no one could prove to the contrary.

He now realized it was dangerous to leave Chieko in Nishi-Okubo and he decided to move her somewhere else.

As Teiichiro anticipated, he was called in by the police numerous times to give testimony. First, there were several visits to the investigation headquarters. Later he was summoned by the public prosecutor's office, then by the Tokyo district court, and finally by the high court.

Kozo Sugiyama had received the death sentence at the district court. He had then appealed to the high court where his sentence was upheld. Now he was appealing to the supreme court.

In the beginning Teiichiro hadn't thought his testimony would be that important to Sugiyama. He never dreamed that it would be on his testimony alone that the man would be sentenced to death. As the case progressed, however, it became obvious that Sugiyama's defense rested solely on Teiichiro's word.

If he had testified that he did meet Sugiyama at Nishi-Okubo on the night of December fourteenth, Sugiyama would surely have been acquitted. But Teiichiro never wavered. His story remained the same to the end.

As he kept repeating his story, he gradually became more proficient in telling it, until he reached the stage where he half believed that he had been at the movies on the night in question.

The victim had been attacked from behind and strangled. She had been seen at the neighborhood shops just before nine o'clock, and the body had been discovered by her husband when he came home at 9:30, placing the time of death in the thirty minutes before the body was discovered.

The inside of the house didn't seem to have been disturbed, but 500,000 yen and an expensive camera were missing. Unfortunately, however, the police were unable to find any fingerprints on the scene that didn't belong there.

As a result of their investigations, the police located the missing camera in a second-hand shop in Ueno. The person who had brought in the camera had filled out a receipt, and although the name and address were obviously false, his handwriting was an important piece of evidence.

While making inquiries in the neighborhood, the police learned that an insurance salesman in the area had been acting a bit suspiciously, and after checking with the insurance company Sugiyama's name had come to light.

Sugiyama had visited the victim's house several times in the past when she was alone, so he knew both her and the layout of her house. On top of this, without Ishino's corroboration, he didn't have an alibi for the time in question.

He claimed to have gone to Nishi-Okubo to visit one of his policy holders, but finding no one at home he had returned to Omori without meeting anyone else. By way of proof he claimed that he had met Teiichiro Ishino in the street, but Teiichiro had denied this.

The owner of the camera shop positively identified him as being the one who had brought in the stolen camera. First the shop owner had said that he resembled the man, but as the case continued, he became more positive in his statements.

Two handwriting experts agreed that Sugiyama's handwriting and the handwriting on the camera-shop receipt were the same.

There being no fingerprints on the scene of the crime meant that there was no clinching evidence. In addition, the police hadn't been able to find any trace of the missing 500,000 yen; they assumed that Sugiyama had managed to spend it all in the two weeks preceding his arrest. Finally, Sugiyama didn't have an alibi for the time when the camera was sold at Ueno.

So Teiichiro's evidence was of crucial importance. In fact, it was a matter of life and death for Kozo Sugiyama.

Ishino's testimony was so clear, so convincing, that no one even suspected that he was lying.

JUDGE: "Does the witness know the defendant?"

TEIICHIRO: "We're not what you would call friends, but he lives in the neighborhood and we generally exchange greetings when we pass in the street."

JUDGE: "That means you would recognize him?"

TEIICHIRO: "Yes."

JUDGE: "The defendant claims he met you at a little after nine o'clock on the evening of the fourteenth of December at Nishi-Okubo, Shinjuku. Do you have any recollection of such a meeting?"

TEIICHIRO: "No, I never met him in that area. At the time in question I was at the theater in Shibuya watching a movie."

JUDGE: "At exactly what time were you watching this film?"

TEIICHIRO: "I was in the theater from approximately seven thirty to nine forty. It was a double bill and I saw both films before returning straight to my home in Omori."

JUDGE: "Did you meet anyone you knew at the theater?"

TEIICHIRO: "No."

JUDGE: "Approximately how many people were in the cinema that evening?"

TEIICHIRO: "I didn't take that much notice at the time, so I may be wrong of course, but I think it was quite full."

JUDGE: "Could you give the court some idea of the plots of the movies you saw?"

TEIICHIRO: "Certainly. In the first film the scene opened on . . ."

In this manner Teiichiro bluffed his way through the investigation headquarters, the district court, and the higher court without being found out. The defense counsel and the district attorney had both questioned him minutely on some points, but Teiichiro had easily managed to deceive them. He seemed almost like the captain of a ship, steering it through a storm, and the passenger on board this ship was Chieko Umetani.

The case was finally taken to the supreme court, but this didn't really make any difference to Teiichiro. By now his testimony had been taken down in writing and was on file in the courthouse. This record made his personal appearance no longer necessary, so Teiichiro was once again free to continue his life as if nothing had happened.

But he couldn't stop his conscience from troubling him.

His testimony was nothing but a chain of lies, and the judge, prosecution, and defense were just rearranging these lies to suit their purposes.

No one ever doubted his story, and the only one except Chieko who knew it was false was the defendant, Kozo Sugiyama.

But Sugiyama was not the only person who knew Teiichiro was lying. There were also some of the neighbors who lived near the murdered woman, the camera dealer, and the handwriting experts. All had lied, intentionally or not, and together had condemned an innocent man.

Teiichiro realized now that life is full of traps and one never knows when one is likely to be caught. In fact, he felt that it was he and not Sugiyama who was the real victim of circumstances. By being in that place at that time on that day, Sugiyama had in fact threatened Teiichiro's privacy and security. If they had never met, Teiichiro wouldn't have suffered the great stress of testifying over and over in court. If he had only stayed with Chieko for a few more minutes, or left a little earlier, or smoked one more cigarette, he would never have been seen by Sugiyama. The difference of two or three minutes, even of one minute, had changed his fate, and he couldn't help but feel how unfair it was.

He saw how the Fates wove their threads and how by falling into their pattern, one's whole life could be changed. Just thinking of it filled him with fear, and he realized how dangerous it is for men even to leave their homes and walk in the street.

A few months later an article appeared in the newspapers reporting that the final verdict on the Sugiyama murder case would be reached soon. Not having had to make any further appearances in court, Teiichiro had almost been able to forget about the case, but the months had left their mark on him.

It wasn't until the end of this time that he learned that Chieko had another, younger lover.

One day, while she was with her other lover, Chieko was reading about the Sugiyama case in the newspaper and indiscreetly had told her lover the truth about that night.

"I feel sorry for that Mr. Sugiyama, you know, he's really innocent," she had said.

When her lover asked her what she meant, she had tried to pass if off, but finally, after making him promise not to tell a soul, she had told him how Ishino really had met Sugiyama at Nishi-Okubo on the night of the murder.

The young man listened to the story in surprise and of course he hadn't been able to keep quiet about it for long. He soon told a friend, and eventually the story came to the ear of the defense counsel who promptly had Ishino charged with perjury.

The secret life that Teiichiro had tried so hard to hide suddenly came to light, and the catastrophe he had tried so desperately to avoid engulfed him.

Teiichiro hadn't had the slightest suspicion that Chieko had another lover all the time he had known her, and it was her deception, her lying to him, that led to his final doom.

# The Woman Who Took the Local Paper

## by SEICHO MATSUMOTO

Yoshiko Shioda sent in her money to the Koshin newspaper for a subscription. This newspaper company is located in Kofu city, which is about two hours by express train from Tokyo. Although it is a leading paper in that prefecture, it is not sold in Tokyo, and if one wants to read it, one has to become a subscriber.

She sent the money by registered mail on February 21 and enclosed the following letter: "I would like to subscribe to your newspaper. Enclosed is my payment. The serialized novel, *The Brigands*, in your paper looks interesting and I want to read it. I would like my subscription to begin from the issue of February 19th."

Yoshiko Shioda had seen the Koshin newspaper only once before. It had been at a small restaurant located in a corner of a building in front of Kofu station. The waitress had left the paper on the table while Yoshiko was waiting for her order of Chinese noodles. It was a typical local paper, with rather old-fashioned type, very provincial actually. The third page was devoted to local news. A fire had destroyed five homes. An employee in the village office had embezzled six million yen of public funds. The construction of an annex to the primary school had been completed. The mother of a prefectural assemblyman had died. That sort of news.

At the bottom of the second page there was a serialization of an historical novel. The illustration showed two samurai warriors engaged in a sword fight. The author was Ryuji Sugimoto, a name unfamiliar to Yoshiko. She had read about one-half of the serial episode when her noodles were served and she put the paper aside. But first Yoshiko wrote down in her notebook the name and address of the newspaper and publisher. She also remembered that the name of the story she had been reading was *The Brigands*. Under the title there was a notation that it was the 54th installment of the serial. The newspaper was dated the 18th. Yes, that day had been the 18th of February.

It was about seven minutes before three when Yoshiko left the restaurant and walked around the town. The square in the middle was crowded with people. Above their heads fluttered white banners printed with the words: *Welcome Home, Minister Sato*. A new cabinet had been formed the previous month and Yoshiko realized that the name on the banner was that of a local diet member who had been appointed one of the new ministers.

Then suddenly there was a stirring in the crowd and the people became agitated. Some of them cried, "Banzai!" A great clapping arose. People who were walking some distance away ran to join the crowd.

The speech began. A man had mounted a platform and his mouth was moving. The winter sun struck his bald head. A large white rose was pinned to his breast. The crowd became silent but at times the applause was thunderous.

Yoshiko looked around. A man standing near her was also

watching the scene and he too was not listening to the speech. He seemed to have his way blocked by the crowd.

Yoshiko stole a look at the man's profile. He had a broad forehead, sharp eyes, and a high-bridged nose. There had been a time when she had thought of them as an intelligent brow, trustworthy eyes, and a handsome nose. But that memory was now an empty one. The spell the man held over her, however, remained the same as it had been before.

The speech ended and the minister descended from the platform. The crowd began to disperse. An open space appeared in the crowd and Yoshiko began to walk. The man also began to walk away—with another person.

The Koshin newspaper arrived five days later. Three days' issues came together. There was a polite note thanking Yoshiko for her subscription.

As she had requested, the subscription began with the issue of the 19th. Yoshiko opened it. She turned to the local news. A robbery had occurred. Someone had died in a landslide. Dishonesty had been exposed in the Farmers Cooperative. Elections for assemblymen had begun. There was a large photo of Minister Sato in front of Kofu station.

Yoshiko opened the issue of the 20th. There was nothing special in it. She looked at the issue of the 21st. Here too there was only the usual news. She threw the papers into the corner of the closet. They could be used later for wrapping paper.

The newspaper arrived by mail daily after that. Her name and address were mimeographed on the brown kraft-paper wrapper. After all, she was now a monthly subscriber.

Every morning she went to the mailbox in the apartment house to get her paper and slowly read it from beginning to end. There was nothing which attracted her special attention. Disappointed, Yoshiko threw the papers in the closet.

This was repeated for ten days. And every day she was disappointed. In spite of this, she was always filled with anticipation before cutting the brown wrapper.

On the fifteenth day a change occurred. It wasn't an article in the paper but an unexpected postcard she received. The card was signed by Ryuji Sugimoto. Yoshiko remembered seeing that name somewhere. It wasn't someone close to her, but she had a clear recollection of it.

Yoshiko turned the postcard over. The handwriting was almost indecipherable, but managing to read it, she immediately knew who it was.

"I understand you are reading my novel, *The Brigands*, which is being serialized in the Koshin newspaper and I would like to thank you for your interest."

No doubt someone had told the author that she had subscribed to the paper because she wanted to read his story. The author had evidently been touched and had sent a card of thanks.

It was a small change from the daily newspaper routine. It was something different, however, from what she had expected. She hadn't been reading the novel—like the handwriting on the postcard, it was probably poor.

But every day the paper arrived promptly. Of course, this was only natural because it had been paid for in advance.

One morning, nearly a month after she had subscribed to the paper, she glanced over the various items of local news. The head of the Farmers Cooperative had fled. A bus had fallen from a cliff and fifteen people had been injured. A mountain fire had destroyed three acres. The bodies of a man and woman who had committed suicide had been found at Rinunkyo.

Yoshiko read the report about the double suicide. The bodies had been discovered in the forest in Rinunkyo. The person who had found them was an inspector of the Forestry Bureau. Both bodies were partly decomposed. It was about a month since death and the bodies were partially skeletonized. Their identity was still unknown. The valley, with its crags and deep gorge, was famous as a suicide spot.

Yoshiko folded the paper, lay down, and pulled the quilt up to her chin. She gazed at the ceiling. This apartment was old. The boards in the dark ceiling were on the verge of rotting. Vacantly Yoshiko continued to stare.

In the following day's paper there was a report on the identity of the dead couple. The man was a 35-year-old guard at the Toyo Department Store in Tokyo; the woman, aged 22, was a clerk at the same store. The man had a wife and children. It was seemingly an ordinary, run-of-the-mill case of double suicide.

Yoshiko raised her eyes from the paper. Her face was devoid of expression—emotionless and at the same time, peaceful.

Three days later she received a postcard from the circulation department of the Koshin paper.

"Your subscription has ended. We hope you will renew your subscription to our paper."

Yoshiko wrote back: "The novel has lost its interest for me and I do not wish to continue my subscription."

On her way to the club, where she worked as a hostess, she mailed the postcard. As she walked on, it occurred to her that the author of *The Brigands* would probably be disappointed. "I shouldn't have written that," she thought.

Ryuji Sugimoto read the subscriber's postcard which had been forwarded to him by the Koshin newspaper and it displeased him considerably.

This subscriber was the same person who had taken the paper because she had found his novel interesting. At that time too the paper had forwarded her letter to him. He was sure he had sent her a note of thanks. But now she was saying that the novel had lost its interest, so she was discontinuing her subscription.

"These women readers—they're so fickle," Sugimoto said angrily.

Since *The Brigands* was written for a mass market, the primary purpose had been pure entertainment; nevertheless, he had taken considerable time and care in writing it, and was confident it was not hackneyed or dull.

Sugimoto laughed bitterly, but gradually he became angry again. He felt as though he were being made a fool of. As a matter of fact, the story was better now than when she had first expressed a desire to read it because it was "interesting." The plot was now more complicated and the characters were engaged in a series of colorful encounters. Even he was pleased with the way the story had developed. He expected it to be well-received, and that was all the more reason he found this capricious woman so annoying.

"This is really unpleasant," he thought, and for two days he couldn't rid himself of the bad taste in his mouth. On the third day the hurt had faded, but it still remained in his subconscious. Occasionally it would flicker through his mind. Because he had worked so hard on the story, he felt worse than if a professional had criticized him. Besides, even though it might seem exaggerated, he felt he had lost prestige with the paper.

Sugimoto shook his head, stood up from his desk, and went out for a walk.

"That woman began to read my novel in the paper midway. Now, where did she first see it?"

The Koshin newspaper was sold only in Yamanashi prefecture, not in Tokyo. So she couldn't have seen it in Tokyo. Therefore, that woman named Yoshiko Shioda, of Tokyo, must have been in Yamanashi at one time.

If that was so, there was no reason why a person who had taken the trouble to subscribe to a paper because she had found the serial interesting would have dropped her subscription after one month. Especially since the novel was undeniably more interesting now than before.

The more he thought about it, the odder it appeared. Obviously the real reason for subscribing to the paper was not to read his novel. She must have used that as an excuse; she was really looking for something else. And because she found it, she no longer needed the paper.

Sugimoto rose from the grass and hurried home. Ideas were whirling through his head.

When he got home, he took the original letter from Yoshiko Shioda out of his file.

"I would like to subscribe to your newspaper. Enclosed is my payment. The serialized novel, *The Brigands*, in your paper looks interesting and I want to read it. I would like my subscription to begin from the issue of February 19th."

The handwriting was neat and precise. But that was beside the point. The puzzling thing was why she specified that the subscription should start two days prior to the date of her letter. In quick cases, newspapers carry news of the previous day. The Koshin did not publish an afternoon paper. Therefore, if she wanted to get the paper from the 19th, it meant she was looking for news of something that had happened from the 18th on.

He had copies of the paper which the company sent him daily. He opened them on his desk. Starting with the one dated February 19, he looked carefully through it. He read the local news and, just to be sure, he also looked at the tourist ads.

He decided to limit his search to something which would connect Yamanashi prefecture with Tokyo. He looked at the various items. During the month of February nothing fitted into this category. He started going through the March papers. Up to the 5th there was still nothing. The same through the 10th. The 13th, the 14th. Then, on the 16th, he found the following story:

"On March 15, at two o'clock, a member of the Forestry Bureau discovered the bodies of a man and woman who had committed suicide. The bodies were partly decomposed and it has been about one month since the time of death. The man was wearing a gray overcoat and navy suit and was approximately 37 years old. The woman had on an overcoat of large brown checks and a suit of the same color and was about 23. The only thing found was a handbag with women's cosmetics in it. It is assumed that they were from Tokyo because a round-trip ticket from Shinjuku to Kofu was found in the woman's bag."

The identity of the couple appeared in the next day's paper. "The man found at Rinunkyo was a guard at the Toyo Department Store, named Sakitsugu Shoda (35) and the woman was Umeko Fukuda (22), a clerk at the same store. The man was married and had children."

"This is it." Sugimoto uttered the words without thinking. There was nothing else to link Tokyo and Yamanashi. On seeing this paper, the issue of March 17th, Yoshiko Shioda had decided to stop her subscription. There was no doubt in Sugimoto's mind that this was the reason she had started taking the local paper. It was the type of news that would hardly have appeared in the Tokyo metropolitan papers.

"Wait a minute, though," he thought.

Yoshiko Shioda specified that the paper was to start from February 19th. The bodies were discovered on March 15, approximately one month after the deaths. Therefore, the suicides had occurred around February 18. Time-wise, it tallied. *She knew about this double suicide.* She subscribed to the paper so she could learn when the bodies were discovered. But why?

Ryuji Sugimoto suddenly found himself becoming deeply interested in Yoshiko Shioda.

He studied her address on the postcard that had been forwarded to him. . . .

Three weeks later Ryuji Sugimoto received an answer to his inquiry from the private detective agency.

Ryuji Sugimoto read the report twice and thought to himself, "When they put their minds to it, they do a remarkable job. They certainly managed to find out a lot, even that Yoshiko Shioda and Sakitsugu Shoda had been having an affair."

There was now no doubt that Yoshiko Shioda was somehow involved in the double suicide of Sakitsugu Shoda and Umeko Fukuda, and that therefore she knew they had committed suicide in the forest at Rinunkyo. One took the Chuo Line to Kofu to get to Rinunkyo. Where had she seen them off? At Shinjuku station in Tokyo or at Kofu station?

He thumbed through the train schedule. He saw that there were about 20 special express and express trains from the Shinjuku Terminus to the Kofu district daily.

According to the private investigator's report, Yoshiko had left her apartment that day at around 11:30, so it was fair to assume that she had gone on the one o'clock special express Azusa #3 which reaches Kofu at 2:53. From Kofu station to the scene of the suicide at Rinunkyo, by bus and on foot, would have taken a full hour. Shoda and Umeko, the suicide couple, would have finally reached the fateful spot just as the winter sun was about to set. Before his eyes, Ryuji Sugimoto could visualize the figures of the two in the craggy ravine, surrounded by woods.

Until their decomposed bodies were found approximately a month later, and the news was reported, only Yoshiko had known about them. She had been reading the local papers to learn when the deaths would come to light. Just what was her part in the whole affair?

Once again he went through the February 19th issue of the Koshin paper. Landslide. Dishonesty in the Farmers Cooperative. Election of town officials. There was nothing exceptional. There was a large photo of the local diet member, Minister Sato, in front of Kofu station.

Sugimoto pushed aside the manuscript, which was due the next day, and holding his head in his hands, he sat, sinking deeply into thought. He never dreamed that one reader's rejection of his novel could have involved him in detective work like this. . .

Yoshiko was one of several hostesses at the Bar Rubicon, a club in the Shibuya district. She was busy taking care of customers when one of the girls said to her, "Yoshiko, someone is asking for you."

Yoshiko stood up. She went to the booth and there sat a plump man of about 42, with long hair. She had never seen him before and he was not a regular of the club.

"You're Yoshiko Shioda?" he asked with a smile.

Yoshiko had not changed her name on coming to this club, but when the man addressed her by her full name she was surprised. In the dim indirect lighting, even though there was a lamp on the table with a pink shade, she searched his face, but she could not remember having seen it before.

"Yes, I am. And what's your name?" asked Yoshiko, seating herself beside him.

"Let me introduce myself," he said, taking a slightly bent name card from his pocket. When she saw the name, Ryuji Sugimoto, printed there she gasped.

Watching her face closely, he said, with a little laugh, "Yes, I'm the fellow who is writing *The Brigands* which you have been reading. The Koshin paper told me about your subscription and I dropped you a note of thanks. I happened to be in your neighborhood yesterday, so I stopped by your apartment. You were out but I was told you worked here. So tonight I came here—I wanted to thank you in person."

Yoshiko thought, "Is that all? So he was just curious. I never read his story seriously anyway. What a character to be so pleased by one person's interest in his story!"

"Oh, how kind of you to take the trouble, sir. I've enjoyed your novel so much," gushed Yoshiko, moving closer to him.

"Don't mention it," replied Sugimoto good-naturedly; then, looking around him, he remarked, "This is a nice club." Next he looked at Yoshiko sheepishly and mumbled, "You're a beautiful girl."

With a sidelong glance at him Yoshiko poured beer into his glass and smiled. "Really? I'm so happy you came tonight. You can stay a while, can't you?"

So he still believed she was reading his novel. He couldn't be a very popular writer if he made such a fuss about meeting one of his readers. Or maybe he was impressed because she happened to be a woman.

Sugimoto evidently couldn't drink very much because after one bottle of beer he became quite flushed. Of course, Yoshiko was drinking too, and several of the other hostesses had joined them, so by this time there were half a dozen bottles on the table, as well as some snacks.

The girls kept calling him "sir," which evidently pleased him, and he stayed for more than an hour.

Just after he left, Yoshiko noticed a brown envelope on the cushion where he had been sitting. She picked it up, and thinking it was his, went to look for him; but he was nowhere in sight.

"He'll be back. I'll just keep it for him," Yoshiko thought and slipped the envelope into the bosom of her kimono, completely forgetting about it.

She became aware of it again after she returned to her apartment. As she undid her obi, the brown envelope fluttered to the floor. Remembering, she picked it up. There was nothing written on the outside of the envelope. It was unsealed and seemed to contain only a newspaper clipping. She decided to look at it.

It was a newspaper clipping about a quarter of a page in size and neatly folded. Yoshiko unfolded it and her eyes widened in surprise. It was the photo of Minister Sato in front of Kofu station, the photo from the Koshin newspaper.

Over the dark crowd were several white banners. The minister could be seen above the heads of the people. It was a scene that Yoshiko had actually witnessed, exactly as it was in the photo.

Yoshiko stared into space. Her hand shook slightly. One of the cords of her kimono still hung loosely from her waist.

Was this just a coincidence? Or had Ryuji Sugimoto intentionally left it in the club for her to see? Her feet were tired, so she sat down on the floor. She didn't even bother to put down her sleeping mat. What did Sugimoto know? She began to feel that he had left the envelope for some special purpose. Her intuition told her so. This was no coincidence. No, it certainly was no coincidence.

Ryuji Sugimoto, whom she had taken to be a pleasant popular novelist, suddenly began to appear in an entirely different light.

Two days later Sugimoto showed up at the club again and asked for Yoshiko.

"Why, good evening, sir," she smiled, sitting beside him; but her face felt stiff.

He smiled back and he didn't look at all like a person with an ulterior or sinister motive.

"You forgot this last time you were here." Yoshiko took the brown envelope from her handbag. The smile remained on her lips, but her eyes watched his expression closely.

He took the envelope and put it in his pocket. There was no change in his expression, but for a moment his narrowed eyes seemed to glint as he met her gaze. Then he quickly looked away and raised the foaming glass of beer to his lips.

Yoshiko felt restless, nervous, and apprehensive.

The relationship between Yoshiko and Sugimoto deepened quickly after that. On the days when he didn't come to the club, she called to invite him. She also wrote to him, not the usual letters a hostess would write to her customers to solicit their continued patronage, but very personal letters.

Anyone looking at them would assume theirs was an intimate relationship. Considering the actual number of times he came to the Bar Rubicon, the liaison formed swiftly. Proof of how far it had developed was shown one day when Yoshiko approached Sugimoto, saying, "Couldn't we go away somewhere together? I could take a day off."

Sugimoto looked delighted. "If it's with you, I'd love to. Where would you like to go?"

"Wherever it's nice and quiet. How about some place in Izu? We could leave early in the morning."

"Izu? That sounds better and better."

"Look now, I'm only suggesting a short excusion."

"What do you mean?" he asked in a disappointed tone.

"I don't want to get too deeply involved—not yet. So let's just make this a pleasure trip. To make sure there is no misunderstanding, why don't you invite a girl friend to go with us? I'm sure you have one."

"I won't say that I don't," Sugimoto said.

"I'd like to get to know her. That's all right with you, isn't it?"

Sugimoto frowned.

"You don't seem very happy."

"There's no point in going if I can't be alone with you."

"Oh, please. That can be the next time."

"Do you promise?"

Yoshiko took Sugimoto's hand in hers and drew her fingernail lightly over his palm.

"Okay. If that's the way you want it, that's how it'll be, this time." Then Sugimoto added, "We might as well decide on the date and time now."

"What? Oh, all right. Wait a minute."

Yoshiko rose and went to the Bar Rubicon office to borrow the train schedule.

Sugimoto arranged for a woman editor he knew to accompany them. He didn't give her any special reason. Because she knew and trusted him, she accepted the invitation promptly.

Ryuji Sugimoto, Yoshiko Shioda, and Fujiko Sakata, the editor, arrived in Ito on the Izu Peninsula just before noon. The plan was to cross the mountains from there, over to Shuzenji, and return by way of Mishima.

Sugimoto wondered what was about to happen. He knew there was danger and his nerves were tense. It was an effort to look as though he suspected nothing.

Yoshiko appeared composed. She held a plastic-covered parcel in one hand. It probably contained a lunch she had packed. The three of them looked for all the world as if they were off on a happy picnic excursion. The two women seemed to be getting along fine.

The bus left Ito and began to climb the mountains. As they climbed, the town of Ito looked sunken and small, and before them spread Sagami Bay, the water purplish in the late fall and blending with the clouds in the distance.

"It's absolutely lovely," commented Fujiko.

Gradually the ocean disappeared from sight as the bus crossed the summit of the Amagi Mountains.

"Let's get off here," suggested Yoshiko.

The bus halted at a bus stop deep in the mountains.

Yoshiko suggested that they explore the area and then take either the next bus or the one on to Shuzenji.

"Wouldn't you like to see where this goes?" asked Yoshiko, pointing to a mountain path leading into the forest. She looked cheerful and her forehead shone with perspiration.

In some places the path was deeply rutted. The shades of green of the different trees were breathtaking. The silence was so intense that it was oppressive.

They came to a thicket of shrubs. Here there was a break in the forest and the sun poured down onto the grass.

"We can take a rest here," said Yoshiko and Fujiko agreed with her.

Sugimoto looked around. He realized they had gone deep into the woods. Seldom would anyone come here, he thought. In his imagination he saw the forest in Rinunkyo.

"You can sit here," said Yoshiko to Sugimoto, spreading the plastic wrapper she had undone from her parcel for him to sit on.

The two women sat down on their handkerchiefs and stretched their legs straight out in front of them.

The editor said, "I'm so hungry."

"Then why don't we have our lunch?" asked Yoshiko.

The two women unwrapped the lunches they had brought. Fujiko had made sandwiches. Yoshiko had prepared sushi. These were placed on the ground along with three bottles of fruit juice.

Taking a sandwich, Fujiko said to the others, "Please have some."

"Thank you, I will," said Yoshiko, taking a sandwich, and added, "I made some sushi but as I'm always eating it, I don't care for any now. If you like some, please eat it." She held out the little box to Fujiko and Sugimoto.

Fujiko laughed. "Thanks. Why don't we switch lunches then." She picked up a piece of sushi and was about to eat it.

"Watch out, Fujiko!" shouted Sugimoto, striking the sushi from her fingers. His face had turned white.

"There's poison in it!"

Fujiko looked at him dumbfounded.

Sugimoto stared at Yoshiko's pale face. She looked back fiercely and didn't lower her gaze. Her eyes flashed.

"Yoshiko, this is how you killed those two at Rinunkyo, isn't it? You're the one who made it look as though they had committed suicide."

Yoshiko bit her trembling lip. She looked ghastly.

Stammering in his excitement, Sugimoto continued, "On February 18th you invited Sakitsugu Shoda and Umeko Fukuda to go to Rinunkyo with you. You poisoned them just as you intended to poison us now, then returned alone. No one would have dreamed they had been murdered. That area is famous for suicides, so it was a perfect setup. People would just think, 'What? Another suicide?' and not give it a second thought. That was what you were counting on."

Yoshiko remained silent. Fujiko was staring wide-eyed. It seemed as if the slightest movement would tear the air.

"You accomplished your purpose. But there was just one thing that troubled you," Sugimoto went on. "You were worried about what would happen to the bodies. You left when they collapsed, but you wanted to know the final outcome. Otherwise, you wouldn't have been able to rest, isn't that so? They say a criminal usually returns to the scene of his crime. You chose to do that through a newspaper. Or maybe you were worried whether the police would call it a suicide or suspect murder. But such a trifling incident was unlikely to appear in the Tokyo papers, so you subscribed to a Yamanashi paper, where Rinunkyo is located.

"That was smart, Yoshiko, but you made two mistakes. You thought you had to give a reason for subscribing to the paper. So you said you wanted to read my novel. You shouldn't have done that. That's what made me suspicious. The other mistake you made was in ordering the paper from the 19th. Therefore, I guessed that something had happened on the previous day, on the 18th.

"My inquiries revealed that you hadn't gone to the club that day. Using my imagination along with the facts, I decided that you must have taken the 1:06 express train from Shinjuku. This train arrives in Kofu at 2:53. You would have to go to Rinunkyo from there, but it just so happened that the local diet member, Minister Sato, was making a speech to a throng of people at that very time. This was reported in the paper, with a photo. I was sure you would have seen it. So I decided to test you with that photo.

"I had a private detective investigate you and Sakitsugu Shoda, and it became clear that you and he were involved with each other. And Shoda was also involved with Umeko Fukuda, the other girl. If they were made to look like a double suicide, it wouldn't cause much of a stir. As I became more and more convinced that my reasoning was correct, I purposely left that photo of Sato for you to see. I knew it would make you suspicious of me. In other words, I wanted you to know that I was testing you. It must have made you nervous, and then you probably became afraid of me. Now it was my turn to wait for you to make the next move. You didn't fail me.

"You suddenly became more friendly and finally, this invitation today. You insisted I bring a girl along. That's because if I were found dead by myself, it wouldn't look like a suicide. If Fujiko and I had eaten your sushi, the poison you put in it would have acted immediately. You could have left us here. Three minus one—that would leave another couple in the mountains of Izu who had evidently committed double suicide. People would be shocked to learn that we two had been so intimate. My wife would probably hide my ashes in a closet."

Suddenly a laugh erupted. Yoshiko Shioda threw back her head and laughed. Then, just as suddenly, the laughter died and Yoshiko spoke sharply.

"I must say, you really are a fiction writer! You couldn't have made up a better story. So you claim that this sushi is poisoned?"

"Yes, I do."

"Then let's see if it will kill me. I'll eat it all myself. Watch me. If there is poison in it, it should take about three or four minutes to kill me. If it's a slower-acting poison, I'll be in agony. But leave me alone."

Yoshiko took the box of sushi from the shocked Fujiko and began to stuff the food into her mouth.

Sugimoto watched fascinated. He couldn't utter a sound.

There were seven or eight pieces of sushi in the box. One by one Yoshiko chewed them and swallowed.

"There, I ate them all. Thanks to you, I'm full. Now we'll see if I drop dead."

And so saying, she lay down full length on the grass.

The warm sun played on her face. Her eyes were closed. A nightingale was singing nearby. Time passed. Sugimoto and Fujiko didn't say a word. More time passed.

Yoshiko seemed to be sleeping. She didn't stir. But, from the corner of her eye, tears made a track down her cheek. Sugimoto was tempted to speak to her, but at that moment she jumped up. It was like a spring uncoiling.

"It's been long enough," she said, glaring at Sugimoto. "If the sushi had been poisoned, I would be dead now, or in agony. Yet here I am, perfectly normal. Is this proof enough that you've let your imagination run away with you? You should be more careful about making such wild claims!"

So saying, Yoshiko collected the lunch box and bottles and tied them up into a parcel, stood up, and shook the grass from her skirt.

"I'm going back. Goodbye."

Yoshiko strode back down the path. Her step was firm. Soon her figure was lost in the tangle of branches.

Sugimoto received the following letter from Yoshiko Shioda.

"You were completely right. I did do it. It is true. I am the person who killed those two people at Rinunkyo. Why did I do it? Well, there was no other way, was there? It was just the usual story of a man and two women.

"The way he died is just as you deduced. When I invited the two of them to go with me to Rinunkyo, Shoda was delighted at the prospect of such a picnic. No doubt it gave him a perverse sense of pleasure to be accompanied by his two mistresses.

"I reserved seats on the 1:16 express from Shinjuku, but I deliberately took the earlier special limited express at one o'clock. I didn't want anyone we might know to see the three of us together. I had about thirty minutes before the other two arrived. During that time I went to a little restaurant in front of the station and had some noodles and that's when I saw your novel in the paper. When I met them, Sato was making a speech in the square.

"At Rinunkyo I gave Shoda and Umeko some sweet cakes that I had made, in which I had put potassium cyanide. They died almost immediately. I got rid of the remaining cakes and returned, leaving the bodies there. Everything went perfectly.

"What a relief! The only misgiving I had was whether the police would suspect murder. Therefore, I decided to take the local newspaper, using your novel as the pretext for subscribing to it. Because of that I ended up arousing your suspicions.

"So I decided to kill you. In the same way I had killed Shoda.

"But you saw through my plan. You suspected I had poisoned the sushi, but actually the poison was in the fruit juice. I thought you would drink the juice after eating the sushi to quench your thirst.

"I brought the bottles of fruit juice back with me. They won't be wasted. I will drink one now . . ."

*Shotaro Yasuoka (b. 1920) is a sensitive author of novels and short stories that are largely autobiographical. To be found in his fiction are references to his unhappy childhood and his poor record as a student. Drafted into the army in 1944, he served a year in Manchuria and was sent home with a serious lung ailment. Illness and poverty were to plague him and his family after the war.*

*In the early 1950s, Yasuoka achieved some success writing short stories; and in 1959, he published a short novel,* A View by the Sea, *now considered his masterpiece. His recurrent theme is the breakdown of the traditional Japanese family and the search for some kind of substitute. Permeating his fiction is a deep sense of rootlessness and the need to find a home.*

A View by the Sea *was translated into English in 1984. Included in the same volume are "Rain" and four other stories.*

# Rain

## by SHOTARO YASUOKA

### TRANSLATED BY KAREN WIGEN LEWIS

Even for a rainy season it had been unusually wet. Though you wouldn't know it from the rainfall totals, it had been coming down steadily day after day, almost without letup.

"Three days in a row," I muttered to myself. There was a heavy object attached to the inside front of my raincoat, pulling the hem down in front and the collar taut against my neck in back; warm raindrops kept rolling along the collar rim to drip at the base of my throat. ——This constant drizzle was more than I could bear. There was a novel I had read once, a story about a man who squandered his life in a romance with some unremarkable woman, but queerly enough one detail that stuck with me was that the main character had been the son of a cleaner. Considering that a man who does laundry for a living spends all his waking hours, year after year, immersed in a cloud of steam from his iron and surrounded by the smell of drying clothes, it seemed not at all implausible for a person born into such a family to come out with a less than resolute sort of personality. As I recall, the famous criminal K_____, who terrorized Japan after the war with a rash of murders in which he would invite a woman shopping and then kill her, came from a launderer's family himself; when you think about it, there's something menacing, some strange atmosphere of fevered passion, that seems to seep out through a cleaner's window, brightly lit as they always are late into the night, and hover over the place making the air there thick and murky. ——The more I thought about it, the more likely it seemed that the unrelenting rain might account for my own bizarre behavior of the past three days. I would have to come up with some daring project, some single ambition with which to pierce my body and soul to the quick. For three days now I had been wandering around town like a fool carrying a hatchet in one hand. I had decided to become a burglar, you see. I say 'like a fool,' but I don't mean to make fun of either my motives or my decision. At the time I had no job, no home, and not even enough money for trainfare to my parents' home in the countryside: there was really no other choice. Besides, I figured the actual work of a burglar could hardly be much of a challenge. If I avoided all the elaborate scheming and plotting typical of detective novels and stuck with a straightforward approach, everything was sure to go smoothly. With an initial resolve and enough persistence to carry it out, the work itself ought to be ridiculously easy.

I originally planned to threaten my victim with a certain knife of mine. I was convinced that this alone, if handled right, would bring about the hoped-for results. But after making one round of my targeted neighborhood I got the feeling this wouldn't do the trick at all. Entering a movie theater in Shinjuku on the way, I thought it over and decided that a weapon of intimidation ought to look like a proper weapon. So from the movie theater I went straight to a cutlery shop. I intended to buy a dagger, one with a birch handle and a blade that shone a dull blue. But as soon as I caught sight of a row of small hatchets designed for chopping kindling wood, I decided to go for one of them instead. I handed over my last 400 yen for it. This was the article I now carried under my raincoat.

The next day I again made the rounds in D_____ town, my targeted neighborhood. But the result was the same as on the day before. All I ended up doing was making repeated comparisons between the gates and walls of a score of houses. But what really depressed me was that, when I decided to start over and had gone back as far as Shinjuku, I walked without thinking into the movie theater that was showing the same film I had seen the day before. More than my own inexcusable carelessness, it was the sight of the same images playing across the same wide screen that really gave me a shock. For some reason I was instantly gripped with terror. I knew then that I was a doomed man. Not only would I fail as a burglar; I would fail at everything I tried. From here on, no matter what good luck might come my way, no matter how easy a road to success might lie open in front of me, I was doomed to falter over some trifle and let the chance slip away from me. . . . The picture on the screen showed a wide expanse of blue ocean. I tried to get up from my seat several times, intending to go back to D_____ suburb. But every time I went to stand up it was as if a wave surged out from the screen and rolled over me, and I kept falling right back into my seat. I ended up sitting in that clammy, broken-down chair until the end of the picture, unable to move.

Today, the third day, the sun had set before I could drag myself out of bed. Since I had carried the hatchet around the whole day before, now when I stood up I got an ache in my left thigh as if someone were jabbing needles into me. If anything, though, this pain became something of an inspiration. I may not have had anything to show for all the walking I had done the day before, but in its own way the sheer determination not to let this pain get the best of me managed to rouse my spirits.

In front of the D_____ town train station was a semicircular pond, the heart of a similarly shaped park from which five streets led out in the shape of a fan. The five streets corresponding to the ribs of the fan were connected by a network of smaller crossroads. I singled out the avenue in the middle, running straight ahead from the station, and resolved to enter the house at the bottom of that street. I had decided that, rather than weigh every factor, it was more important to concentrate on carrying out whatever I made up my mind to do.

A low iron gate hung ajar in the middle of the ivy-covered stone wall. Beyond the gate a massive and imposing pine spread its branches; beyond that I could just see the front door, set into an English style brick entryway. A small green car was parked in the shade of the tree, its wet roof glistening in the rain like the back of a giant beetle. I made my way up the path, crunching gravel under-foot as I went. It seemed an eternity before I reached the door. On the stone patio were two doormats, one of iron and one of woven hemp. I deliberately avoided them both. I rang the bell. Then, to be ready to flourish the hatchet on a moment's notice, I unbuttoned the front of my raincoat, grasped the handle with my right hand, and waited for the door to open. As soon as I heard the lock turn, in an instant I had forced my body through the crack between the door and the jamb, left shoulder first. A sudden smell of mildew made me shudder, and there before me stood a grey-haired, aproned woman, bowing. I gripped the hatchet and took half a step forward.

"Oh!" A soft cry escaped the woman's lips as she raised her eyes. But the uncanny thing was, her expression radiated nothing but peacefulness and calm. She looked to be about fifty. There was actually a hint of a smile on her face, which was now so close to mine that even her light dusting of powder seemed glaringly white. I involuntarily relaxed my grip on the hatchet handle under my raincoat. Just then the woman's eyes went wide with surprise and she said an astounding thing.

"Why, if it isn't the man from the electric company! In that case, why don't you step on around to the back door . . ."

The woman broke off midsentence with a peal of laughter, apparently overcome with the humor of her own mistake.

For a moment I was stunned. By the time I snapped out of it I was standing on the doorstep outside the entryway. I took two or three steps toward the back door and then I was suddenly overwhelmed with a feeling of total foolishness. The woman's laughter still rang in my ears. Despite its apparent spontaneity, some quality in that laughing voice had communicated gentility—there was something shiny about it, as if it had been scrubbed clean with soap—and this left me completely defenseless.

Should I really pretend I was from the electric company and go into the house as she had bidden me to?

I toyed with this notion more out of curiosity than desperation. From the direction of the kichen I caught a whiff of the sweet, heady smell of boiling meat; they must be making some kind of soup. But no sooner had I started to walk towards it than I heard a sudden burst of laughter, presumably from the maids and house-boys, which filled me at once with dread and self-loathing, and I promptly turned on my heels and ran for the gate.

I ran blindly until I came out at a small park. I had made a note of the place before. There was an enclosed spot in one corner that afforded cover on all sides, behind some bushes that fronted the road. . . . Before I had even reached the place, I heard the first raindrops on the leaves overhead; gradually I began to catch my breath.

I sat down on a bench at one end of a pond, full to the brim with muddy water. But this time I was tormented by the question of why I should have been such a coward back there. Who was that woman who had answered the door, anyway? The lady of the house? Then did her apron mean she had guests coming on short notice, I wondered, and was bustling about with last-minute preparations? If that were true, then when I happened to come to the door just then she had mistaken me for her drop-in guest. . . . I was sure the whole household was having a good laugh about me by now. But I couldn't work up any hatred for them because of it. In fact, my memory of the woman's laughter was indescribably sweet. I knew it was silly, but I was starting to picture her as a genuine innocent, a person so pure of character that she would show equal graciousness to burglars and guests alike.

The soup in that kitchen had sure smelled good, though, I mumbled to myself, and I stood up to go. But a stab of pain shot through my right thigh and I fell back onto the bench. I hadn't noticed anything while I was running, but the hatchet I was still carrying under my raincoat must have banged me there repeatedly. Maybe I was imagining things, but at this thought my whole thigh felt suddenly warm and wet. Was I bleeding? The exposed blade of the hatchet could have torn my pants and made a gash somewhere in my leg. Trembling, I took the hatchet out from under my wet raincoat to have a look. The blade lay across my lap like a thing asleep, gleaming dully in the fading light of the rainy dusk. There was no trace of blood, not a nick on the blade.

Though I was relieved, I was irritated with myself at the same time. Everything in the world seemed stupid and infuriating, including me. D_____ town, with its placards hung on every house like little botanical labels; the laughter of that old woman, still ringing in my ears—stupid, all of it. Whatever had possessed me to read a stupid thing like "purity of character" in her, I was sure I didn't know. But my own stupidity was the worst of all. Looking at the hatchet on my lap, I thought again about the panic I had felt while running away just now from that house. Hadn't that been closer to the desperation of a little boy who's been left out of the game than to actual fright? One thing was sure: the mere voices of the household help had frightened me more than any prospect of being arrested and sent to the police.

I would have to start all over from square one. I just couldn't leave it like this.

Following my earlier reasoning, I tried as much as possible to avoid setting up a "plan" ahead of time. The way I figured, if I did try to slap together some kind of scheme, the first thing that didn't go according to my calculations would ruin me. So, abandoning the idea of breaking into a stranger's house, I hid out instead in the branches of the corner thicket to wait for a victim.

But for some reason, as soon as I started waiting the traffic going by the place mysteriously fell off. Of course I had purposely chosen a secluded spot, but at this rate I was beginning to doubt whether anyone lived there at all. Not a soul walked by. . . . Since I was without a watch I'm not sure exactly how much time passed, but I'd say I was there for over an hour, crouching in the bushes in vain.

Maybe I shouldn't have let myself fall into a passive, waiting position.

As I mulled this over I looked across the blank face of a wall of ōya stone barring the view across the street. To one side of it was a concrete wall, and on the other side stood another one of stone, topped by a grassy embankment—honestly, it was as if someone had purposely put them there to try a man's patience. . . . So where was everybody? Surely this was where I had passed that old American woman yesterday, out in the rain walking a dog in a little raincoat; and the day before that I was sure I'd seen a young woman walk by here alone. Was there some awful jinx on me so that for this one day not even a lone puppy dog was to go by?

My boredom finally got the best of me and I stood up half out of my thicket, when suddenly I caught sight of a man coming straight toward me.

Damn. Had he seen me?

Quickly I fell back to my knees. If I had been spotted, it would be better to stand up boldly, but I thought there was a fifty-fifty chance I hadn't been. Though he was heading straight toward me he was still fairly far away, and the light was behind me. . . . On the other hand, there was the man's formal, traditional clothing—a crested kimono over a divided *hakama* skirt, with white tabi socks and wooden clogs; it clashed strikingly with everything in the surroundings. And then, as if I hadn't already had enough surprises, he completely threw me by turning straight into the park. He was mumbling under his breath as he started down a path that passed within six feet of where I was hiding. His head was shaved bare, and seemed to wobble back and forth on his thin neck.

"It's not right, simply not right. . . . I'm sorry, but it's just not right. . . ."

As he repeated these words the man shifted a white bundle he was carrying to the hand that held his umbrella, turned to face a clump of trees, and proceeded to urinate.

"It's not right, it's simply not right. . . ."

Somehow it seemed that he was talking to himself. He looked terribly precarious, standing there holding the bundle and the umbrella with one hand while hitching up the front of his *hakama* with the other, and it made me nervous just to watch him, but I was to be more exasperated still when, after he was through, he continued muttering to himself and showed no sign of going away.

"It's not right—people in this town talk a good line but all they really care about is themselves—whatever happened to religion? What happened to faith? I tell you, this is not right."

Could the man be a Shinto priest? Maybe his bundle was full of oracles and paper charms for selling door to door. If so, there ought to be grounds for a certain camaraderie between us. Instead, his mumbling only irked me the more.

"Here's a fellow with seven children and nothing to feed them— it's just not right, people around here think it's nothing to do with them and won't give a penny to help."

How long was he going to keep this up? Glancing away, I saw a plump, middle-aged woman in a black raincoat walking down the road in front of me, her eyes on the pavement. Here was my chance. I had only to jump out right now and wave the hatchet at her and she was sure to drop her purse and run. . . .

But it didn't take long for it to dawn on me that with that bungling priest here my hands were completely tied. In fact, I'd been wanting to relieve myself for some time now, but had had to keep still because of him. I wondered if I should attack him first; but somehow after listening to his diatribe I couldn't do that either. It wasn't that I felt sorry for him—not in the least: it was rather that simply letting that sullen, under-the-breath muttering fall on my ears had depressed my spirits, sapped my energy, and killed whatever will I may have had to act.

Before long the muttering broke off. But any sense of relief I felt was short-lived. Turning back toward him, I was startled to see that he was bent over a lunch box, eating. At this sight my last hopes were dashed. In the same moment the tension I'd lived with these past three days went slack, and I was sharply reminded that I had had nothing in my stomach since morning.

I was furious with this man. He ate noisily; I could distinctly hear him crunch on a pickled radish, or cough down some crusty piece of cold rice with a scratching sound in his throat like a chicken swallowing its gravelly feed. I very nearly leapt out of the bushes, tore the lunch box from his hands, and hurled it into the mud-filled pond. But just then a gruff voice boomed out of the darkness behind me.

"You there."

It was a policeman.

"Hullo, you there, what are you doing in here. It says in plain

letters right out front, nobody's allowed in the park after dark. . . .
Come on, let's get moving. If you don't get going I'll have
to . . ."

The man made no reply; he only turned around once. He
continued to work his chopsticks the whole time as if he were under
a spell . . . "Oh brother," said the policeman, and he turned and
went away. The man carried on with his meal, completely
oblivious.

I stood up and came out of my thicket. I stopped directly behind
the man, and stood awhile watching him eat. I could see the jaw
bone that jutted out from either side of his thin neck moving
ceaselessly as he chewed. The longer I looked at the exposed crown
and the deeply sculpted back of the man's bald head, the more
murderous I began to feel. A musty smell of radish pickles seemed
to seep from the wrinkled skin just visible above his collar. I could
wait until the moment he finished eating, and then plant my
hatchet right in the middle of that clean-shaven head. Soundlessly I
unbuttoned my raincoat. This time—this time I'd really do it. But
just then the man started mumbling again.

". . . I can't go back like this . . . I can't go back like
this . . ."

Go back where? What did he mean, "I can't go back?" Chances
were he was fretting about not having brought in enough money
today. But to me this thick, low voice, seeming to crawl along the
very earth, suddenly conjured up powerful images of the darkness of
both my ancestral village and my family home, and I felt my grip on
the hatchet start to go limp.

After a brief letup, the drizzling rain must have started falling
again. I could hear droplets hitting the leaves and grass, and
something cold struck my cheek. I took the hatchet firmly in hand
once again and inhaled loudly. But the man went on as before, his
lunch box and chopsticks in hand, muttering over and over to
himself the mournful words. "I can't go back like this, I can't go
back like this."

**Kobo Abe** *(b. 1924) is an avant-garde novelist and playwright who is known for his Kafkaesque style. His early work was called surrealistic, and elements of fantasy are present in virtually all of his fiction. "The Dream Soldier" is one of his most realistic pieces.*

*The great success of* The Woman of the Dunes *(1962, trans. 1964), both as a novel and as a film, made Abe an internationally known figure. He is active in the theatre and some of his plays have been performed in the United States. Once an active member of the Communist Party, he seems to have moved away from politics in recent years. He writes about universal questions, revealing his deep concern about the lack of freedom and the loss of identity in today's complex society. Sometimes labelled an existentialist writer, he also ponders questions about the nature of reality.*

*Several of his novels and a few of his plays have been translated into English. Of interest to mystery fans is his novel* The Ruined Map *(1967, trans. 1969), an offbeat detective story that only Abe could have written.*

# The Dream Soldier

## by KOBO ABE

### TRANSLATED BY ANDREW HORVAT

On a day so cold that dreams froze
I had a frightening dream.
In the afternoon
The dream put on my cap and departed
And I did the latch on my door.

This story took place about fifteen years ago. Although truth is supposed to be timeless, it is time that this story needs the most. Perhaps that is because there is no truth to the story.

Tucked away in the mountains near a prefectural border, the village had been since the night before entirely engulfed in a snowstorm. The wind howled as if in agony. A company of soldiers who from early morning had been engaged in cold endurance exercises made their way from the town over the hills. Dragging their large straw shoes in the deep snow to the tune of a marching song, they crossed the village with unsteady steps, only to disappear like shadows into the snowstorm.

The wind died down at nightfall. In the police substation at the entrance of the village a solitary old police officer was leisurely peeling potatoes while warming the soles of his feet by the heat of a red hot stove. The radio was on, blaring something he wasn't listening to. He was immersed in a series of daydreams.

"There's a thing or two I know about this village. I know that the mayor and his assistant, in cahoots with the head priest, are diligently embezzling the village rations, and they hide everything underneath the temple floor. But I don't say a word. They know that I am keeping quiet. Nevertheless their sending me things, from time to time, isn't so much to shut me up as it is from a feeling of goodwill. If I were to retire I wouldn't have to run like other resident officers. I could even settle down and stay here. Maybe I could get together with a widow that's got some land and pass my last days in peace. As long as you are modest about your needs, there's no better life than that of the farmer. And then, when my son comes home from the army, why I might even have a house to welcome him home with. . . . Thanks to the war, this village has three women landlords. Of course, for the time being there's a son in every house. But who is to say some of them won't give up their lives for their country. No doubt I'll be able to make a nice match. I don't recall having done anything that the villagers could hate me for, and the number of landed widows is steadily on the increase. Now now, hold your horses; no reason to lose your head, just calmly think things out. The size of the paddy fields added to the number of relatives, divided by two. . . ."

Suddenly the telephone rang causing the policeman to drop his half-peeled potato into the ashes. Picking it up, he rubbed it against his shirt-tails; then he stretched himself as if in pain and got down on the earthen floor. Picking up the receiver with the inattentive motions that are typical of his occupation, he began to answer in an unconcerned tone of voice. But his expression abruptly turned to fright and the fingers with which he held the potato began to tremble.

After leaving the village, the soldiers continued to march straight toward the mountains. Along the way, they passed through valleys and forests, practising their high terrain maneuvers. It was well after three by the time they arrived at the last mountain ridge. The wind was raging with yet greater intensity. Although the soldiers could hardly even breathe, they were ordered to return double quick on nothing but their empty stomachs. Despite the stiff punishment that they knew awaited them, six soldiers dropped out of rank. As this was a special exercise to test the effects of exposure to hunger, cold and fatigue, it was expected that some would fall out of rank, and for that reason there was a corps of medics following from behind. Upon returning to base, however, it was discovered that the medics had picked up only five stragglers. One of the soldiers, it seems, had disappeared for good.

The soldier is starving. He'll have to call at the village. But should the villagers lay themselves open to attack he might not stop short of violence.

The old policeman put down the receiver. Drawing up his shoulders, he slowly returned to his place near the stove. He took a noisy breath through his nose and for a while just scratched the top of his balding head. He raised his eyes to look at the clock. It was seven-thirty. He didn't want to move. It was too cold outside. Besides it wasn't clearly a case of desertion yet. At any rate an awful snowstorm was raging. Could it not simply be that he had become separated from his companions and lost his way? It'd be a fool who'd want to desert in weather like this. He'd leave tracks in the snow and they'd catch him for sure. He may have just lost his way. By now he must be frozen stiff. . . . On the other hand, should the wind keep on blowing, the snow might be safer. The wind hides footprints. Then again he may have counted on that. It could have been a premeditated crime. For all that, the wind has died down completely. He may have fallen right into some trap. I guess there's just no successful precedent for crime. . . . I've received a report. But that doesn't mean I've received an order. Anyway, this fellow is under MP jurisdiction, so he's none of my business. Deserters, compared to escaped convicts, are, after all, just well-intentioned cowards. Leave him alone, leave him alone. No good has ever come from butting into other people's affairs. Besides I've never heard of a deserter that's made it yet.

He thought he heard a light tapping on the front door. He turned around quickly. He tried straining his ears for a while but he heard no noise. Maybe he was hearing things, he thought. For some reason, though, he began to feel uncertain about things. It wasn't any usual uncertainty either, rather a feeling so close to fear that he could not explain it to himself. Of course his fear was in no way directed toward the deserter.

Hatred did not usually erupt within him regarding criminals. And because he did not feel this hatred he realized the existence of something which ordered him to hate. This was something he had not been aware of before, being in the secure position of a pursuer. It was only now that he came to peer into the hell that separates the pursuer and the pursued. He stood up. Stricken with pangs of conscience, he tried shouting. "I won't allow it!" he cried out. But then shouting has never been of much use in dispelling uncertainty. This feeling of uncertainty was still only that very tiny inner feeling, because from outside there came a much greater feeling of fear to overwhelm him. The inner feeling was, after all, the uncertainty of being an accomplice. It was a fear that everyone in the village might have felt. But not being able to flee from his uneasiness caused him to sense a yet greater anxiety.

"Well, I guess I am getting too old," he thought to himself. Indignation welled up within him, "When the time comes to settle the matter, it'll be settled. It's not a case of me, myself, alone, bearing all the responsibility." The back of his throat had a strange wet feel to it. He cut off the air that was going to the stove, put on his sword, turned up the collar of his overcoat, and went outside.

The snow was light. It rustled, releasing a pleasant crunch at each step. It's easy to recognize footprints, but it's impossible to tell whether or not they were made by shoes. Immediately upon rounding the corner on which the fish-market stood, he reached the mayor's house. It was the only house in the village equipped with a Western-style window. A bright lamp was burning in it and someone's heavy laughter spilled onto the street. It was the head priest's voice. Instead of going around the back way as he ordinarily might have done, the policeman boldly pulled open the front door.

The atmosphere in the room stiffened as if everyone had been startled. The mayor's dull voice trembled above the sound of chinaware being hurriedly put away: "Who is it? At this hour."

A little too early for fright. The policeman just cleared his throat and purposely refrained from answering. The *shōji* screen opened revealing the assistant mayor's face. "Well well now, if it isn't the resident officer?"

"Come right in, come right up," said the head priest leaning forward. The *shōji* slid right open. All three smelled of *saké*.

"Something awful has happened," the policeman began saying.

"What is it? But save your breath, just step right in and close the screen and have a drink."

"Some soldier's run off to Mount Kita," the officer continued.

"A deserter?" the head priest peered over the edge of his glasses and swallowed the lump in his throat. "If he is going to Mount Kita, then no matter what route he takes, he's got to pass this way."

"That's the message I got . . . and it seems he's aiming at this village."

"Aiming at?" the mayor slid a finger along the ridge of his nose in a somewhat annoyed fashion.

"Yes, and they say he's damn hungry," the officer added.

"That means we're in for trouble."

"Why?" the assistant cut off the mayor in a spirited manner. "Deserters are generally traitors, aren't they? And probably cowards to boot. What's wrong with going up the mountain, hunting him down and catching him?"

"Hold it a minute! He does have a gun. What's more he's hungry, and he might be pretty desperate."

"In China," the mayor sighed, "no matter where you go, they've got castle walls separating one village from another."

"They're not castle walls," the assistant mayor retorted.

"No, those aren't castle walls."

"Those are ordinary mud walls."

"Yes, just mud walls, that's all."

Suddenly they all heard a sound, as of a chain grating. Instinctively, they all turned toward the noise. It was the wall clock just on the verge of striking eight. The head priest impatiently resumed his previous position. "Well then, what are we going to do?"

"Like I said, catch the fellow and tear him to pieces!" There was a good explanation why only the assistant mayor carried on in such a bragging manner. In all the village he was the only man in his thirties who was still not in the army. Even so, compared to his previous outburst, his tone of voice had weakened considerably.

Not wishing to dampen anyone's spirits, the policeman nodded and said, "Yes, by all means, after all the fellow's a treacherous dog. But then again . . ." he lowered his voice and tilted his head to one side, "he does have a gun, and you never can tell what may happen with a hunted down, starving traitor that's got a gun."

"Yes, it's like letting children play with swords." That was the head priest speaking, gesticulating toward the assistant mayor while looking at the policeman's face. "What do you think we should do?"

"What should we do, you say? Well that's . . ." the mayor leisurely let the words slip while holding his nose. "You sure this deserter isn't a fellow from our village?"

"He can't be," the assistant's jaw dropped. "No, a fellow like that's gotta come from some warm, comfortable place," he said in a loud, earnest voice.

"But then why did he decide to desert here, in such a cold climate?"

"Well, for the life of me . . . anyway he won't get away with it . . . feel sorry for his parents."

"Mind you, I heard a story about a widow in some village, and she hid a deserter in her loft for over two months."

"That's an old story! No traitors like that around nowadays."

"Yes, that's right."

"Look at them, all with their hearts in their mouths," the policeman thought to himself. "But I guess anyone else would be frightened under the circumstances. They're afraid of being mixed up with a criminal. Should they find out, though, they won't be able to cover things up without dirtying their hands. If they stopped their ears, their hands would hear the fellow's cries for help. Plugging the ears itself is a sign that one is already an accomplice . . . that is to say, these people are completely in cahoots with each other."

"Well, if you'd like to know my opinion . . ." he said expressionlessly, sucking air noisily up his nose. "I think we should let everyone in the village know, by means of an extraordinary circular or some such thing, that as there is a deserter approaching the village all doors should be securely fastened, no one should even step outside, that just like during air raid warnings no light should be allowed to escape through cracks, and that should anyone ask them anything, they are not to answer. Engaging in conversation means getting involved. For example, first he asks for water. 'Well, if it's only a little thing like that,' and the fellow gives him water. But next it's food, and if the fellow gives him food, next he'll be wanting a change of clothing, and after clothes, it's money. And what's he going to ask for next? He's been completely taken care of, but it's no good, 'cause someone can now recognize his face, so finally, at the end, it's 'Bang!' "

All three held their breaths waiting for the officer's next words, but as there was no indication that the speech would continue, the mayor asked quietly, "And that's it, is it?"

"After that, I suppose the MPs would come in. . . ."

The head priest stretched himself and said, as if the whole thing sounded very unpleasant to him, "I think I should be going. It's pretty far to my place."

As the mayor started hurriedly to phone the militia guard room, the assistant followed the priest and left his seat. "Guess that fellow'll be starting to wander around the village any minute now."

It took less than an hour for the message to permeate the length and breadth of the village. As if a typhoon warning had been announced, every house had its shutters barred, all the weak spots had been boarded up. There were some who even prepared bamboo spears and hatchets by their places of rest. After ten o'clock the whole village, with the exception of the police station, sank into total darkness. An animal-like fear enveloped the place.

Despite their fear, though, most families gradually went to

sleep. Only the old policeman, as if waiting for something, stayed up all night continuing to strain his ears for sounds outside. Of course the villagers, behind their boards and shutters, had no way of knowing. . . .

The next morning, just as dawn was beginning to break, from beyond the hills to the south there came the shrill sound of a train whistle continuing to blow a long time in rapid succession. The foreboding cry streamed unmercifully into the village beneath the low clouds. Most of the villagers woke to its sound. The people who understood what it meant quickly opened their shutters.

The policeman, his eyes bloodshot from lack of sleep, gazed through the south-facing windows toward the hills. His eyes could clearly see the single straight, gray line which extended beyond the hills. The whistle stopped blowing. In a while the assistant mayor, carrying a pair of skis, appeared accompanied by two men. "It seems somebody's thrown himself in front of the train again. I think I'll go and take a look. It might've been that traitor. Want to come along?"

"No, I'd better stay. Could get a call from town."

In no time the three skiers came upon the gray line that extends beyond the hills. Nodding at each other, they began to follow its path. The old policeman finally left the window and crouched in front of the fire.

When the assistant mayor returned he found the policeman dozing in the same position. The assistant tried waiting silent until the old man woke up. Just when he was about to give up, the old man opened his eyes and asked in a whisper, "Well . . . did you get a look?"

"Yes, I sure did."

"Well, then you. . . ."

"You must have known all along?"

"Yes, I knew."

"Then was it you that made him do it?"

"Well, you see . . . I know, you know just how ashamed I am . . . he didn't have to do it so close to the village. It must have been out of spite toward me . . . I can't think of a fellow like that as my son . . . but you might do me a favor and keep quiet about this."

"But the two fellows I went with, they already know."

"I guess you're right. I'll have to take what's coming, won't I?"

"His body wasn't badly deformed or anything. His gun was right beside him, hung on a branch."

"Well . . ."

"By the way, hadn't we better erase the footprints under your window?"

"I suppose you're right."

Ten days thereafter, the old policeman left the village, dragging a small cart behind him.

> On a day so hot that dreams melted
> I had a strange dream.
> In the afternoon
> Only my cap returned.

*Shizuko Natsuki (b. 1938) is Japan's foremost female mystery writer and is sometimes called the "Agatha Christie of Japan." Her first big success was* Disappearance *(1973), which follows a journalist as he investigates the disappearance of a woman who was once his lover. Her 1983 novel* Murder at Mt. Fuji *sold over a million copies.*

*Natsuki can be considered a follower of Matsumoto in that she attempts to enrich the mystery form with social content. Frequently her stories deal with the clash between outmoded traditions and modern realities. She has based some of her mysteries on actual cases, as have other writers in the "social detective" school.*

*In a recent interview, she was asked if she feels comfortable being compared to Agatha Christie. Her response was "No, not at all. . . . Christie's novels don't go into social problems the way mine do. These days, mystery stories have to reflect on real human problems in a way that readers can relate to, so if people feel I resemble Christie—except on the superficial level of being a female mystery writer—I must be doing something wrong."*

*Natsuki's* Murder at Mt. Fuji *was published in English in 1984. Seven of her short stories have been translated: one in* Ellery Queen's Japanese Golden Dozen *(1978), four in* Ellery Queen's Mystery Magazine, *and two in the* Ellery Queen's Prime Crimes *anthologies.*

# The Pawnshop Murder

## by SHIZUKO NATSUKI

"I'll be off then."

Eiko Horikoshi was 42 and the owner of a prospering pawnshop. As usual, she was smiling when she said goodbye to the shop manager, the assistant manager, and the clerk.

"Goodbye," they called to her as they watched her rather plump figure disappear out the door. It was 7:40 and since the Horikoshi Pawn and Loan Shop closed at eight P.M., the young clerk, Naomi, started to put away the gems and watches.

The shop manager, Tsunemoto, was at the counter talking to a young man in a leather jacket who looked as if he were either a student or laborer. The young man had placed a camera on the

185

counter in front of him and Tsunemoto's eyes glinted behind his gold-rimmed glasses as he studied the form the young man had filled in.

Tsunemoto was only 36 years old and already manager of the shop. He was shrewd and energetic, contrasting strongly with the assistant manager, Tsuji, who was never likely to rise above his present position.

"How much were you hoping to get for this?" the manager asked, picking up the camera and looking at it closely.

"I thought you might be able to give me about forty thousand yen."

"No, I can't give you that much. You see, they've stopped manufacturing this model and that reduces the value considerably. I can offer you fifteen thousand—that's my best offer."

After a few minutes of haggling the young man settled for the figure that Tsunemoto offered, and thrusting the fifteen thousand, minus one month's interest, in his jacket, he slouched out.

On one of the walls of the shop was a placard giving the rates of interest on the loans from five thousand to five million yen, the rate becoming smaller as the loan increased in size. Being in a good location near one of Tokyo's larger railway stations, the Horikoshi Pawn and Loan Shop catered to a much better class of customer than its competitors in the suburbs and dealt mostly in share certificates, jewelry, and other small but valuable items.

Above the notice of interest rates, in a position that made it easy to see, was a list of the shop's rules:

*Highest prices paid for popular items and easily disposable merchandise.*

*Lower prices paid for hard-to-sell items.*

The shop itself was small, about sixteen square yards in size, with a counter running across the width of it near the door; the back part served as the shop's strongroom.

"I've got to go over the ledgers tonight," Tsunemoto said as Tsuji and Naomi struggled to close the shop's heavy shutters. Looking up, they could see his tall skinny form in front of the open door of the strongroom.

This vault was only about six square yards in size and two of its walls were covered with shelves filled with TVs, cameras, golf clubs, mah-jongg sets, and various other items people had pawned. Beyond another thick door set in the rear wall of the strongroom was another strongroom of about the same size, this one lined with cabinets containing the more valuable items—stock certificates and all kinds of jewelry.

When Naomi and Tsuji locked up, both of these doors were open; but this was not unusual as Tsunemoto often stayed late to check the items in the strongrooms against the shop's ledger.

Tsuji said goodbye and hurried off, and Naomi, after going back inside for her bag, soon followed. Being next to Tokyo's Ikebukuro Station, land was at a premium and the surrounding buildings all huddled close to each other. The entrance to the pawnshop was in a gloomy alleyway. The building opposite was a windowless, rather seedy, 24-hour coffee bar where about six months before, the customers had all become unconscious from the lack of oxygen.

Naomi had graduated from a high school in Saitama prefecture the previous year, and although she had wanted to enter a bank or a large financial company, the competition for that kind of position had been too much for someone of her easy-going nature, and she had ended up at Horikoshi's. While she was still at school, she had dreamed of being a career girl in one of the large companies, but she had been at the pawnshop for a year now, and often she heaved a sigh of disappointment as she walked out of the shop into that stuffy, dirty alleyway.

She was complaining to herself as she closed the shop's stainless-steel door when she suddenly stopped with a cry and crouched back toward the entrance.

Somehow the middle finger of her left hand had got caught in the closing door and it hurt so much that for a minute she could hardly breathe.

Gradually the pain subsided, and then giving another sigh of dejection, she turned toward the station.

It was now the middle of October, and as she walked she could feel the cold seeping through the soles of her shoes. She had a date with her boy friend Kumazaki at the coffee bar near Shinjuku Station at 8:30.

Kumazaki, far from being the glamorous businessman of her dreams, was a freelance reporter who had made friends with her after frequent visits to the pawnshop. He was a large-boned hirsute young man and generally he took Naomi out to dinner and the movies about twice a month and seemed serious in his intentions toward her.

Naomi hurried to her date.

The next morning Naomi arrived at the pawnshop a bit later than usual, turning into the alleyway that led to the shop at about 8:40. The shop opened at nine o'clock, but Naomi had to be there by 8:30 in order to tidy up first. When there had been a second girl in the shop, they had taken turns coming in early, but since the other clerk left, Naomi now had to work longer hours.

Halfway down the alley she saw Tsuji standing round-shouldered in front of the steel door of the shop, fumbling in his pocket for his key. Tsuji always arrived at exactly 8:40, regular as clockwork.

Hearing footsteps behind her, Naomi turned around and saw Eiko Horikoshi step into the alley; she was wearing a bright blue suit.

"Good morning, Ms. Horikoshi," she said. "You're early today."

Eiko had lived alone in an apartment in Mejiro since her husband died and usually she visited her other shop before coming to the Ikebukuro branch. As a rule she didn't arrive in Ikebukuro until about eleven o'clock.

Giving Naomi a vague answer, Eiko hurried on to the shop. She looked worried, and there was something about her manner that made Naomi quicken her pace to where Tsuji had finally succeeded in finding his key.

He put the key in the lock and tried to turn it.

"That's strange," he said, shaking his head in disbelief. "The door isn't locked."

Twisting the knob, he pushed and the stainless-steel door swung back.

"I suppose Tsunemoto must have forgotten to lock it last night."

"Maybe he's still here," Eiko said quickly. "I had a call from his wife this morning."

"His wife?"

"Yes, she says he never came home last night but that when she rang the shop, no one answered."

Inside it was pitch-black; the shutters on the windows were still down.

Tsunemoto's shoes were lying by the entrance.

Tsuji hurried to open the shutters. By the light that came in through them and through the open door they could see an empty noodle bowl on the counter. There was nothing unusual in this as it was obviously one from the shop where Tsunemoto always ordered noodles when he worked late. What was odd, however, was that nowhere in the cramped interior of the pawnshop was there any sign of Tsunemoto himself.

No, it was too early to say that; there was still the strongroom in the rear; its door was closed.

Eiko went to Tsunemoto's desk, and opening the top drawer, took out a key attached to a large wooden tag. This was the key to the nearer strongroom—the key Tsunemoto was supposed to take home with him at the end of each working day.

Eiko looked over at Naomi and Tsuji for a moment, then walked over to the door of the strongroom.

To open the strongroom one had to first put the key in the lock, dial the combination, then turn the key. The only people who had access to the key and knew the combination were Eiko and Tsunemoto.

Eiko set the combination, turned the key, and then, with Tsuji's help, pulled the heavy door open.

Inside, the lights were on and the door separating the two strongrooms was open, allowing them to see through to the farther room.

Both rooms seemed to be in a disorderly state, with one of the drawers in the jewelry case half open, and a watch from the shelf lying on the floor. In the nearer of the two strongrooms one of the golf bags had fallen over, and lying beside it as if embracing it, lay Tsunemoto. Seeing his pale and twisted features, Naomi felt faint, remembering the occasion when several people had almost died of suffocation in the coffee bar across the alley.

"It is clearly a case of suffocation. Due to the strongroom being perfectly fireproof, once the door is closed no air can circulate at all."

Detective Inspector Danto explained to Eiko in a deep, rich voice what must have happened. The police still hadn't finished their investigation, but Tsunemoto's body had been taken away to the morgue. The body had already been cold when it was discovered, and the ambulance men could do nothing but confirm that the shop manager was dead.

"There have been a lot of cases like this recently. Why, not so long ago there was that affair in the coffee bar across the way."

In this accident five people, including the staff, had suddenly collapsed in the windowless room. Another customer, seeing what was happening, managed to crawl to the telephone and call for an ambulance before he too became unconscious. Luckily, all the people involved recovered after a couple of days in the hospital, and the police recorded it as an accident. It had been late at night and the customers had been there for several hours. With no one going in or out, the door had remained closed, and before long all the air in the room had been exhausted.

"Nobody died that time, but in the same month two seamen on a Chinese ship in Kobe harbor suffocated after the hatches were closed on them. And a ship's hold is much bigger than this strongroom of yours."

Inspector Danto had been in charge of the investigation at the coffee bar and he seemed to have developed a special interest in this kind of case.

"By the way, when you all went home last night at about eight o'clock, was Mr. Tsunemoto already working inside the vault?"

He looked beyond Eiko to where Tsuji and Naomi were standing.

"That's right," Tsuji answered in a strained voice.

"And where was the key to the strongroom at that time?"

"I suppose it must have been in Mr. Tsunemoto's desk, as usual."

Generally, Tsunemoto would open the first strongroom with his key when he arrived just before nine o'clock. However, the middle door—the door between the two strongrooms—was never opened until Eiko arrived at eleven o'clock. The farther strongroom held the more valuable items and certificates, and only the owner was in possession of that key.

To lock either vault, though, no key was necessary. Anyone could lock the doors; all that was needed was merely to push them and twirl the combination locks. During business hours the key to the first strongroom was kept in Mr. Tsunemoto's desk, and the combination lock of that door being left open, one had only to turn the latch to open the door.

"Does that mean that the door could have closed of its own accord while Mr. Tsunemoto was working in there? After all, it's impossible to open the door from the inside even when it's only on the latch."

"Of its own accord? No, I don't think so. The door is much too heavy to move by itself."

Eiko, Tsuji, and Naomi all said the same thing.

"I think it's impossible that someone could have locked him in by mistake. You see, there is an emergency alarm which you can ring from inside the farther vault. But being night-time, not even that could help poor Mr. Tsunemoto." Eiko's voice was subdued.

"What? You mean you've got an alarm system?"

"Yes, last month someone got locked in a butcher's refrigerator and died. When I read about it in the papers, it gave me the idea, so I had the alarm bell installed."

The button was fitted in the corner of the rear vault, and when pressed it rang a large alarm bell in the shop. When the police pushed the button, however, nothing happened, and after checking the wires, they found they had been cut by a pair of wirecutters just where the wires entered the room.

It was then that the police first considered foul play, and when Eiko checked the contents of the vaults, it was found that two valuable rings, one diamond and one ruby, were missing. It suddenly became very likely that while Tsunemoto was working alone the night before, someone had broken in, held up the manager, probably with a gun, taken the two rings from the farther strongroom, and locked Tsunemoto in when the intruder left. After that the criminal had cut the wires leading to the bell and escaped into the night.

"I wonder how long the air lasted," Eiko said.

And I wonder what time he was locked in, Inspector Danto thought, before answering Eiko.

"How long the air lasted? That can easily be determined from the autopsy. We can check the time he had his noodles delivered, then work out when he died by seeing how far the noodles were digested."

He glanced over at the bowl on the counter, then continued, "If we know what time he died, I think we can calculate when he was locked in by checking on his respiration rate and the amount of oxygen available in the room. I've never heard of a case of this type before, but luckily one of the assistant professors of forensic medicine at J University specializes in cases of suffocation. I think we will probably go to him for help."

This was assistant professor Miyahara. Even Naomi knew his name since he had been interviewed by the newspapers after the accident in the coffee bar. In the article, reference had been made to his experiments with rats which enabled him to calculate to a very narrow margin the length of time a human being could live in a fixed area before exhausting the air.

"We can be sure that Mr. Tsunemoto was all right at eight o'clock last night, but just in case, I'd like to know what you were all doing last night."

So saying, he glanced over the three people in front of him. Suddenly his eyes were caught by Naomi's middle finger—the nail was bruised and the rest of the finger was swollen.

"How did you hurt your hand?" he asked.

"Oh, that. I caught it in the door . . . over there."

Naomi half turned in panic and indicated the steel door to the shop.

"When was this?"

"Last night, as I was leaving."

"You said you left with Mr. Tsuji last night. Didn't you?"

"Yes, but I was a few moments behind him and I hurriedly closed the door—"

Naomi's voice grew smaller until she broke off in mid-sentence. Both Eiko and Tsuji were staring at her hand with horror, as if this was proof that Naomi had slammed the door on Tsunemoto and had caught her finger in it.

"The people from the Kiyoken noodle shop stated that Tsunemoto ordered the noodles at eight-fifteen and that they were delivered at about eight-thirty. Therefore, if one assumes that he ate them straight away, according to the amount of digestion and various other body functions, he must have died at about two o'clock in the morning."

Naomi was telling Kumazaki everything she had learned from detective Danto's second visit. Kumazaki had been to Sendai on business the morning the murder was discovered and it wasn't until six o'clock the following day that Naomi had finally been able to get in touch with him. After she told him what had happened, they arranged to meet as soon as she finished work at Horikoshi's.

"Since they have a reasonably accurate time of death, Danto says that they're going to ask professor Kazutoshi Miyahara at J University to give them the approximate time the crime was committed."

"Time of the crime?" Kumazaki asked. He was 27 years old, well built, dark-skinned, and always looked unshaved. His voice was his best point, though, being soft and cultivated, and not matching his looks at all. When he had come to Horikoshi's to pawn his watch or tape recorder, it had been this gentle voice that had first attracted Naomi.

"Yes, the time that the door was closed. You see, once the door was closed, he wouldn't be able to get any fresh air."

"Oh, I see. Have they come up with an answer?"

"It seems to have been very difficult. They say the professor worked all night and even made another series of experiments with a rat."

To begin with, the police calculated the volume of the two strongrooms. The center door divided the space into two rooms of almost exactly the same size, each room being 5 feet wide, 10 feet deep, and 6 feet 6 inches high—or a volume of 325 cubic feet. At the time of the crime the middle door had been open, which meant that there was a total of 650 cubic feet. The main problem, however, was that both rooms had many articles in them. The farther room was lined with drawers for the jewelry and stock certificates, while the nearer was filled with TV sets, golf bags, and other goods. After these had all been measured, it was discovered that they accounted for about 20 percent of the total volume, leaving 520 cubic feet, or 14.4 cubic meters of air.

Professor Miyahara used these figures in attacking the problem, taking into account both the physiological and physical data he had learned from his experiments.

"He says that the average adult male inhales four to five hundred milliliters of air with each breath, but of this one hundred to one hundred and fifty are expelled again without being used by the body. The same adult will, on the average, breathe approximately twelve times a minute, but this depends on the temperature and the amount of exercise done by the subject. So, considering all this, the air in the strongrooms could have lasted from four to six hours."

"Does that mean that even with five hundred and twenty cubic feet of air you can only live for four to six hours?" Kumazaki asked.

"Yes, the tests they made with rats all gave the same result. They put rats in all sizes of glass tanks and measured the time it took for them to struggle and collapse. However, as they didn't know how much air a rat breathes, they made several experiments measuring the size of the rat and the container, and then correlated this with the known facts about humans."

In the case of the rats, when they were put in a case five times the size of their bodies, they lived for approximately 45 minutes. When they were placed inside a case ten times their size, they managed to survive for two to two and a half hours. No matter how many times the experiment was repeated, they all lived for this length of time.

Therefore, if one takes a man to have a mass of 0.7 to one cubic meter, he should be able to live for about two hours with seven cubic meters of air, and for more than four hours with fourteen cubic meters of air.

Detective Danto had explained all this in detail, not only because he was interested in it professionally, but because he wanted to hear the alibis of all the staff.

Professor Miyahara's results were almost exactly the same as those that had been published in the newspaper after the accident in the coffee bar, and they all admitted having read that account.

"Tsunemoto died at two in the morning, and as the crime took place four to six hours earlier, it means it happened between eight and ten in the evening."

"But he had the noodles delivered at eight thirty, didn't he?"

"Yes, we checked the staff at the noodle shop again, but they all stick to their original testimony. They did add, however, that after he took the noodles he was heard to lock the shop door on the inside."

This meant that Tsunemoto must have known his murderer. The door was fitted with a peephole and it would be extremely unlikely that he would have opened it to a stranger at that time of night.

"The detective said that it could possibly have been an outsider, but since the murderer had been inside the vault and knew all about the bell, he suspects us most of all."

Naomi sounded quite upset.

"That means it's likely that between eight-thirty and ten o'clock someone from the shop went back and killed Tsunemoto."

"Yes, that's why they asked for all our alibis."

The previous day, the police had heard their alibis, but as they weren't sure at what time the crime had been committed, they hadn't gone into much detail. Now, however, that they knew the murderer had acted between eight-thirty and ten o'clock, they concentrated on that period.

"I told them I was here with you nearly all the time in question."

Naomi looked around the dark interior; the juke box was pounding out music at high volume.

"That's true," Kumazaki said, "but unfortunately the police never put much faith in alibis provided by friends."

"And I don't think it's very likely that the waitress will remember us," Naomi added, sounding even more depressed.

Naomi wasn't the only suspect. Tsunemoto, being in the kind of business he was, appeared to have made many enemies. When loans were overdue, it wasn't unusual for him to go to the debtors' companies and demand payment, thus making his customers lose face in front of their colleagues.

Then again, it was possible that Tsunemoto had often accepted stolen goods, and discovering them to be so, had threatened the thieves with the police.

There were rumors at the shop that Eiko and Tsunemoto had had some kind of personal relationship, and after his death these rumors had been repeated until even Tsuji seemed to suspect Eiko. One day he said to Naomi, "If you ask me, I don't think the boss could have opened the new shop at Ekoda if it wasn't for Tsunemoto's skill in business. I can't help thinking that between them they managed to pull the wool over the tax office's eyes and make a lot of money on the side. If that was so, the boss wouldn't have wanted him to talk about it.

"You must have noticed how Tsunemoto was becoming rather swell-headed recently, treating the shop as if it were his own, and I suppose he was getting in the boss's way."

However, both Eiko Horikoshi and Tsuji had sound alibis from eight-thirty to ten.

On the evening of the murder Eiko had left the Ikebukuro shop at 7:40 and gone by car to the other shop at Ekoda where she arrived at 8:15. She had stayed there until she went back to her apartment at Mejiro a little before eleven, and her late husband's parents, as well as staff members who lived behind the shop, were willing to testify that she hadn't left earlier.

Tsuji had gone to a bar with two friends and stayed until 10:40, after which he had gone home, in the housing project at Takashimadaira.

The only one in the shop who didn't have a firm alibi was Naomi.

That evening a new lead turned up. Tsunemoto's wife discovered that the notebook her husband always carried was missing from his effects. His wife lived in Fujimidai with their young son and she had been going through his things after the funeral. She phoned the shop to see if the notebook was there, and Naomi answered her call.

"Yes, it was a slightly large, brown leather notebook. My husband always carried it in his back pocket and would make all kinds of notes in it. He was a very methodical man, you know. Anyway, I'm sure he had it with him that day when he left for work."

Naomi was certain she remembered having seen the brown notebook. In fact, she was sure she had seen it in Tsunemoto's back pocket as he stood in front of the nearer strongroom when she went home that night. When the body was found, however, although the ledger was standing on one of the shelves, there was no sign of the notebook.

Tsunemoto's wife also got in touch with the Ikebukuro police station and on hearing about the book, the official inquiries took a different turn.

Wasn't it likely, while he was locked in the vault, that Tsunemoto would want to write a dying message?

If one assumed he knew who was responsible for taking the rings and locking him in the vault, it would seem quite logical that after trying to open the door and pushing the button of the emergency bell, he would want to tell others who was killing him. The best way to do this would be to leave a note, and where better to write it than in the notebook that he used numerous times each day.

The murderer must have come to realize this and returned to the vault later to retrieve the notebook before anyone else could see it. Returning to the scene of the crime would have been easy if, after locking Tsunemoto in the strongroom, the murderer left the combination lock where it was and knew where the key was kept.

Once this new development occurred, it became necessary to check the alibis of all the suspects from ten o'clock onward. This cheered up Naomi. After she had left Kumazaki, she had gone to visit a friend at Akabane. She had arrived at 10:30 and stayed until morning. Her friend and her friend's sister who shared the apartment both swore that it would have been impossible for Naomi to have left their apartment during the night.

Neither Eiko Horikoshi nor Tsuji could supply the police with a firm alibi for the time after two in the morning. Tsuji had been with his family, he said, but that didn't give him a strong alibi, and Eiko had been on her own since she left the Ekoda shop at eleven.

But Naomi didn't feel relieved long. The police next considered the possibility that Eiko and Naomi had worked together. They thought that Eiko had bribed Naomi to lock Tsunemoto in the safe and then Eiko had come back and taken the notebook. Naomi could tell what they were thinking because the questions from Inspector Danto became more and more to the point.

However, Naomi knew better than anyone else that she was innocent and therefore she didn't really suspect Eiko either. Why, even Kumazaki could have done it. He was a regular customer at the shop and knew the layout; he could have committed the crime before he arrived at the coffee bar that night. After all, he had been a little late. But Naomi hated herself for even suspecting him; she realized that the strain must be getting to her.

Two days later Kumazaki phoned Naomi, sounding very excited and saying that he had a new theory about the case. They arranged to meet at a coffee bar, and when Naomi arrived late, he seemed hardly able to master his impatience and started talking right away.

"This case is unusual in that the time the crime took place and the time of death are separated by several hours. In order to pinpoint the time that the crime took place, it was necessary to calculate back from the time of death, and using a very complicated system at that."

"That's right," Naomi said. "When they had the accident in the coffee bar opposite, the same idea came up and we discussed it a lot at work."

"Professor Miyahara's calculations were published in the papers, weren't they? I think that whoever did this must have read that article and calculated that Tsunemoto could live for only four to six hours in the vault. But even though it was very likely that Professor

Miyahara would be called in to give his opinion, the criminal can't have been sure that the results would be the same."

"But it must have gone according to plan—I mean that's how the murderer was able to arrange an alibi," Naomi said. "Tsunemoto was locked in four to six hours before he died, which means he was locked in between eight and ten o'clock, and anyone who has an alibi for that period is in the clear."

"Of course," Kumazaki said, "I'm not going to say that Professor Miyahara is wrong, but what if the crime didn't happen the way the police think it did? That would make all their calculations worthless."

For a moment Naomi held her breath in excitement. This was the first time someone had looked at the case from another angle, and it may be that Kumazaki had found the blind spot in everyone's reasoning.

Kumazaki sat deep in thought and she watched him as he put some sugar into his cold coffee and started stirring it.

"You said that the boss put the emergency bell in the vault last month, didn't you?"

"Yes, she thought of it after she read about a butcher's boy being locked in the refrigerator by mistake."

"Are there any other pawnshops with a similar alarm in their strongrooms?"

"Not that I know of. There are several with burglar alarms under the counter, but the workmen who put in the bell all laughed and said we must be the only pawnshop with one. But the boss was insistent. She said that it must be put in right away before she forgot about it."

"Maybe she had it fitted especially for the murder."

"What? In order to cut the wires?"

Kumazaki nodded to indicate that she was on the right track.

"But it would only go to prove that the crime was committed by someone in the company who knew about the alarm."

"No, not only that."

"But what other effect would it have?"

The two of them stared at each other, both engrossed in this line of thinking while they sipped their coffee.

"Seeing that the wires had been cut, what did the police think? They supposed that they had been cut in order to stop anyone hearing the bell and rescuing Tsunemoto, and this would mean that Tsunemoto could have gotten into the rear vault to press the button."

"Yes, but he would be able to push it, wouldn't he? After all, it isn't as if he had been knocked unconscious before he had been locked in, and when I went home that night I saw that the door to the rear vault was open. The next morning when we found the body, that door was still open, so—"

"Yes, and on top of that, the wires had been cut. It makes it obvious that the middle door had been open all the time. But maybe that was the reason why the bell was fitted in the first place— to reinforce that idea."

"Do you mean that the middle door was not open?" Naomi's voice quavered. "That it was *closed*?"

"Try looking at it this way. If the middle door was closed from the time that Tsunemoto was locked in until he died of suffocation in the front vault, *he would have had only half of the air.* That means he would have died *in two to three hours, not four to six hours.* This means that the crime was committed not between eight and ten, but *between eleven and twelve o'clock.*"

Naomi closed her eyes and tried to work it out.

Suppose that while Tsunemoto was working late that night, he had a call from Eiko Horikoshi asking him to stay until she could come over.

Eiko left the shop in Ekoda before eleven, and could easily have got to the shop in Ikebukuro by 11:30. After she arrived she would have entered the near vault with Tsunemoto and after locking the middle door would have waited for the chance to lock him in. This would mean that Tsunemoto would have only two or three hours of air, although, as the front vault held the larger articles, it was probable that he had even less.

Eiko would have calculated that he would be dead by two in the morning, and gone back to her apartment until then. When she returned to the shop, she would have knocked on the nearer door, and having made sure that she got no reply, opened it. Tsunemoto would be lying on the floor beside the golf bag, his face contorted with agony, and next to him would be his notebook.

After opening the middle door with her key, Eiko went in and took the two rings to make it look like the act of a burglar, and as she left, she would have noticed any message in the notebook and taken the notebook with her.

After cutting the wires leading to the bell, she departed, leaving the outside door unlocked.

In this way, when the body was found the next day with the middle door *open*, it was certain the police would estimate that it took the manager four to six hours to die, thus setting the time of the crime at between eight and ten o'clock, a time when Eiko had a perfect alibi.

If one looked at the case this new way, it made the people with alibis for the eight-to-ten period seem the most suspicious. Naomi now realized she had figured out the truth: Eiko was the murderer. Confirmation? While anyone could close the door of either vault, *only Eiko could reopen the middle one.*

At about ten o'clock, when the phone boxes in the coffee bar were empty, Kumazaki nodded to Naomi and they both got up.

They went to the phone in the farthest corner and Naomi, picking up the receiver, dialed the number of the Ekoda shop, knowing that Eiko had gone there to do the day's paperwork. Kumazaki stood behind Naomi, using his body to screen her from the rest of the coffee bar.

The phone was answered.

"Hello, Horikoshi here." Eiko's vigorous tone came from the receiver.

"Is that you, Ms. Horikoshi? It's me, Naomi."

Naomi licked her lips nervously before continuing.

"It's about Mr. Tsunemoto's accident. I have just remembered something important that I didn't tell the police. I am going to call them now, but I thought I should get in touch with you first."

"Something important?" Eiko was almost whispering.

"Yes. On the day he died, Tsunemoto was already in the strongroom checking the goods against the ledger when I left. The thing is that when I looked, the middle door was closed and he said something about only checking the front vault.

"When we found the body though, the middle door was open and the whole thing just slipped my mind when the police questioned me."

"Rubbish, the middle door was open all the time!"

"Oh? How did you know that?"

"I—I—it was open when I left."

"But I was the last one to leave that day—apart from Mr. Tsunemoto, of course—and the door was closed then."

"But it can't have been—"

Eiko stopped in mid-sentence as if she realized that it wouldn't do to press the point. Then she continued in a cool voice.

"Are you sure you haven't made a mistake, Naomi?"

"Yes, I'm sure. It was something the detective said when he was interviewing me today that reminded me. He said that he couldn't find Tsunemoto's fingerprints on the button of the emergency bell in the far room and they thought this was a bit strange."

"His fingerprint on the bell?" Eiko murmured as if she had been taken by surprise.

"Anyway, I'm going to the Ikebukuro police station now and I'll tell them all I know."

Naomi paused, then strained at the earpiece; but all she could hear was the sound of Eiko's breathing. Just as she looked up at Kumazaki's tense face, Eiko started to speak.

"I'd like to talk to you first—before you go to the police."

Naomi nodded to Kumazaki. She would go to a dark, quiet place to hear what Eiko had to say, but he would be hiding nearby and would be a witness to everything that was said.

# The Sole of the Foot

## by SHIZUKO NATSUKI

Toho City has a population of approximately 35,000 and is situated only about one hour from Tokyo by train. It is a quiet town, surrounded on three sides by mountains, and its main claim to fame is the Rinko Temple which was built there some four hundred years ago.

Since the town was connected with Tokyo by a private railway line and a national highway, the number of pilgrims visiting the temple has increased tremendously each year; most of them go on to spend the night at a nearby hot-spring resort area.

The temple itself consists of several large wooden buildings set among the trees on a heavily wooded mountainside. Here and there the white concrete walls of new buildings can be seen contrasting sharply with the mellow wood of the original structures.

The main hall of the temple is dedicated to the Buddhist god of success while the secondary shrine is dedicated to Daikoku, the Shinto God of wealth. The presence of these two gods is obviously the reason for the temple's huge popularity, and in these days of inflation the temple is always crowded with merchants and office workers who come to pray for prosperity.

The temple is especially crowded on New Year's Day when people come from far and wide to partake in the famous ceremony at the Daikoku shrine. A similar ceremony is conducted at many Shinto shrines, but the one at Toho City is by far the most famous. The pilgrims give a small amount of loose change to the priests who wash the coins in the temple's stream and return them to the donors. It is said that if a man keeps money blessed in this way for the remainder of the year, the god of wealth will smile on him.

After the ceremony the pilgrims move on to the main temple to make an offering to the Buddha of success before setting off home, and so popular is the event that on the first and second of January the main street of the town is overflowing with cars and gaily clad people on their way to and from the temple. There is another flurry of excitement on the second and third of May when the spring festival takes place, but for the remainder of the year the town is a quiet, peaceful place far removed from the bustle of city life.

Friday the eighth of December had been a cold day with heavy snow clouds filling the sky. Although it didn't usually snow in this area, this day was bitter cold and a few lonely snowflakes drifted down from the mountain's peak behind the temple.

It was the first really cold day that winter and because of the inclement weather there was hardly anyone in the main street that afternoon when three men robbed the local bank.

The bank was an unprepossessing concrete building set in the middle of the main street, looking more like a post office than a bank. Although the shutter over the main entrance was closed at three o'clock, the employees' entrance, which opened onto a side street, was left open to cater to anyone who hadn't been able to visit the bank by the official closing time.

At 4:15 that afternoon one of the clerks noticed a youngish man look in from the side door, but he soon disappeared and the clerk didn't give him a second thought, believing the man was one of their regular customers who had forgotten something and would soon be back.

There were seven people employed in the bank, two girls and five men, but two of the men were out on business and wouldn't be back until about six o'clock when the building would be locked up for the night. All the employees had alarm switches under their desks which connected directly with the police station; but there were no customers in the bank and they were quite unprepared when three men in black ski masks burst in through the side door.

The first man rushed up to the nearest clerk and covered him with a shotgun, while the second seized one of the women clerks and held a hunting knife to her throat. It was all over in a few moments and no one had a chance to react.

"One move from any of you and I'll blow this man's head off!"

The robber with the gun had a deep voice, but it was muffled by his ski mask.

"If anyone calls the police you're all dead!"

Apart from the girl who was being held by the knifeman, they all had risen to their feet involuntarily, but seeing that the intruders weren't bluffing, no one made an effort to press the alarm.

The man with the gun nodded to the third member of the gang, a big man who had been standing unarmed by the counter. Seeing the signal, the third man put his gloved hand into the pocket of his jacket and produced a small bottle and a handkerchief which he folded into quarters. He pushed his way behind the counter and going up to one of the clerks, told him to put his hands behind his back. As soon as the bank employee complied, the robber opened the bottle and everyone in the building could tell from the pungent smell that it contained ether.

Pouring some of the liquid onto the handkerchief, he put the bottle down on the desk, and standing behind the clerk, clamped the material against the man's mouth and nose. The clerk struggled briefly, but the big masked man held him firmly and in less than a minute the clerk slumped to the floor unconscious. The robber then moved on to drug the girl who was sitting at the next desk.

The remaining gang members continued to guard their hostages and in less than five minutes only the three robbers and the manager were left conscious. The man with the gun, who seemed to be the leader, walked over to the manager and prodded him in the chest with the gun.

"Where's the money?" he demanded.

The manager saw that any resistance would be futile and gestured sullenly toward the safe behind him. The main door of the vault was open, and all that stood between the holdup men and the money was a light mesh door. The gunman ordered the manager to open this and the manager, drawing a large bunch of keys from his desk, did as he was told.

The safe contained about twenty million yen in cash, approximately one hundred thousand dollars, and after gazing at it rapturously for a few moments, the leader nodded toward the big man who lost no time in administering the drug to the manager.

The three men then stuffed all the money into a large knapsack that the knifeman had been carrying, and slipped out through the side door to a small gray car they had left outside. The whole robbery had taken less than ten minutes and the robbers had disappeared in the direction of the temple long before anyone knew that anything unusual had happened at the bank.

It was 5:20 before the police were informed of the robbery. The girl who had been threatened with the knife was the first to regain consciousness and as soon as she had her wits she pressed the alarm.

The men from Toho police station soon arrived on the scene, and once they learned what had happened, they set up roadblocks on all the roads out of town and arranged for checks at the bus and railway stations. This having been done, they started their inquiries in and around the bank. The other bank employees regained consciousness, and after a brief checkup at the local hospital, were declared to be unharmed and fit to help the police investigation.

No clues were found in the bank: the robbers hadn't left

anything behind and having worn gloves the whole time, they didn't leave any fingerprints. The only possible clue was a number of large footprints in front of the teller's counter which were thought to have been made by the robbers' rubber boots; but no one could be sure the prints belonged to the thieves, and besides, they weren't very clear. The police weren't sure they would even be able to trace the manufacturer.

The interrogations of the clerks didn't help much either. None of them had seen the robbers' faces except for the moment when the first man had looked in through the side door; but he had only stuck his head in briefly—too short a time for the clerk to see him clearly. Both the man with the gun and the man who had administered the ether had been above average height, especially the latter of the two, and the clerks all guessed that he must have been at least six feet tall. The man with the knife didn't have any particular distinguishing features, being of average height, and like the others clothed in dark-brown baggy clothes.

The big man with the drug had come the closest to the clerks and two of them had been able to state that he had a gold tooth; but despite the fact that he and the gunman had spoken, their voices had been muffled by their masks and no accurate description of their voices was possible.

With only this to go on, the police realized they would have to be lucky if they were to capture the gang, and although someone reported seeing a small dirty-gray car parked outside the side entrance of the bank, the person had not made note of the car's license number. Even if he had, the police doubted that it would help much; a gang that had planned everything else in such careful detail would not be likely to have forgotten to change the license plates on their escape vehicle.

Lieutenant Sato of the Toho City police force and Lieutenant Kaizuka from the Prefectural Headquarters were in charge of the inquiries at the bank, and after they had searched the place thoroughly and questioned the witnesses, they made their way back to headquarters to discuss the case with their colleagues. They were still a bit early for the meeting, so they decided to go up to the canteen and have a cup of tea while they waited.

"We were called in too late. The alarm didn't go off until five twenty which means they'd already been gone an hour before we knew what had happened and could set up the roadblocks."

Kaizuka looked a bit vexed when he said this.

"Yes," Sato said irritably, "and what's more, the men on the roadblocks didn't even know what color car they were supposed to be looking for! Anyway, with an hour's lead I doubt that they'd be anywhere in the area. It's a classic case of locking the barn door after the horse has been stolen."

"Yes, the whole thing was executed beautifully from the beginning. Whoever planned the job must have been quite familiar with the bank to have timed it for four fifteen, because while the side door would still be open, it was very unlikely there would be any customers an hour after the bank had closed. On top of this, they still had an hour and a half before the rest of the bank staff returned, and so they kept the number of people they would have to deal with at an absolute minimum. Also, on that particular day the bank had been asked to hold eighteen million yen in readiness for the local businesses' and shops' payday and therefore had twenty million on hand in its vault."

"Yes, they certainly planned it well, but we've still got one lead."

"You mean the serial numbers on the notes?" asked Kaizuka, nodding.

They had learned from the manager that while ten million yen had been in untraceable used notes, the remaining ten million yen had been in new notes, and there was a record of the serial numbers.

When all the others got back to the station, they discussed the case and decided on the following courses of action:

1) Try to find witnesses and discover what happened to the gray car.
2) Investigate everyone who purchased ether recently.
3) Check up on all the employees of the bank and anyone else who might be familiar with the inner workings of the bank.
4) Investigate everyone in the prefecture who had a shotgun license.

5) Announce in the papers that all the stolen money was untraceable, then have all the financial institutions in the area keep a check on the serial numbers.

Sato wasn't very optimistic—he felt there were too few clues. They had no way of tracing the car and anyone could easily have bought the ether at a pharmacist's long ago. There were at least fifteen thousand people in the prefecture with shotgun licenses and no doubt many more who owned guns illegally. The only possible chance Sato could see was to trace the robbers through the serial numbers on the notes.

That year the weather during the New Year's holiday was exceptionally good and Rinko Temple had a record number of visitors.

Two hours before the bell that rang in the new year had finished tolling, there was already a long line of people waiting by the small river for the money-washing ceremony. As the day wore on, the road from the temple down to the main street of the town was jammed with cars, mostly from Tokyo, and the sidewalks were crowded with family groups and people wearing kimonos.

The bank was closed, and with its shutters down it looked like any other building, but some of the passers-by had obviously read about the robbery and could be seen standing outside looking at it.

According to a police estimate that was published on January fourth, there was a record 1,700,000 visitors to the temple during the three-day holiday. The local newspaper also went on to estimate that there was probably more than one hundred million yen given in offerings.

Considering that most of it was given in loose change, this was a huge amount, and every year the offerings were counted by the temple's staff in a basement room under the main building. The workers, all wearing white-paper masks over their mouths and noses, would count all the notes by hand while the coins were separated by a machine hidden in the bottom of the offertory box and arrived in the basement sorted into their different values. The head priests checked the money in person, and when the totals were known, they were recorded in the temple's ledgers as the temple's chief source of income. After the holidays the local bank sent an armored car to the temple, and after rechecking the money in front of the temple staff, the messengers took the money away to be deposited. Temples in Japan represent a great deal of business to the banks, so Rinko and the other main temples all receive special treatment from the financial institutions.

About ten days later, after the festivities were finished and the town had sunk back into its usual peaceful routine, the police received a telephone call from a local bar at a little after eleven in the evening. Apparently a 10,000-yen note whose serial number corresponded with that of one of the stolen ones had turned up. This was the first lead they had received and as soon as he heard about it from the officer who took the call, Sato hurried out to verify the report.

The call had come from a bar called Fuji which was in a small building just off the main street about a mile from the bank. It had been built about ten years before and was already beginning to show signs of age. It had a counter and three tables with an old-fashioned jukebox set against the back wall. It did a brisk business at the New Year when the town was filled with tourists, but usually it was only frequented by a few of the town's younger citizens.

Although the serial numbers hadn't been published in the papers, as time passed the police decided not to rely only on the banks, but also to get in touch with the bars, supermarkets, and other places that dealt daily with money.

The Fuji landlord, Chino, was standing behind the counter, a garish cravat in his collar which clashed with his shirt. He had the 10,000-yen note laid out in front of him and looked very pleased with himself.

"I've been very careful to check all the ten thousands I've taken in ever since the police told me about them."

Sato took out his notebook and checked the number against his list. There was no mistake—it was one of the stolen notes.

"I generally look after the till myself in the evenings," Chino continued. "So when Mr. Suzuki gave me this note I automatically checked the number and saw it was one of the ones on the list!"

"What? You know the name of the man who gave you this?"

"Yes, he's one of my regular customers, that's why I was so surprised. But anyway, as I was saying, when he gave it to me there were still some other customers on the premises, so I waited until I closed up for the night before I called you."

Suzuki was a man of about fifty who lived near the bar. He came in alone four times a month and after having two or three whiskies, he would pay in cash and go home. This routine had been going on for years, so the landlord had got to know him by name.

"He's not much of a talker, but I think he said that he worked at the temple."

Apart from the office workers who commuted to Tokyo every day, many of the residents of Toho City worked for the temple in one way or another.

Investigation revealed that the note passer's full name was Toshiro Suzuki; he was fifty-one years old, and although he had been working at the temple as a clerk for twenty years and was now head of the general affairs section, he was not a priest. He lived in a small bungalow a few hundred meters from the Fuji bar with his wife Miyako, forty-seven, and his son Shigeru who was thirteen and attended the local junior high. The house was small, but Suzuki had had it built to order a short time before on some land his wife had been given by her family who were local farmers.

The police learned that Suzuki was a serious and methodical worker, but was also quiet and introverted and wasn't good at making friends.

Forty-one people were employed full-time at the temple. Nineteen were priests, twenty were laymen, and an old couple acted as caretakers. Apart from the bishop and two young novices, the monks had charge of the various buildings and helped with the business side of the temple. The laymen were all under the deacon, and although Suzuki was chief of the general affairs section, he wasn't particularly intelligent and didn't stand out among his colleagues.

The police also investigated Suzuki's financial position. Although he had recently had a new house built, he still had a tidy sum in the bank; also, his wife had some money of her own and they had only one child. None of this was particularly unusual. In fact, compared to the priests of the temple who all lived in luxurious homes and drove to the temple in expensive limousines, Suzuki's lifestyle was very modest.

He left his house at 7:45 every morning and walked down the main street for five minutes to the temple. In the summer he would return home at 5:30 and in the winter at 4:30. He didn't seem to have any hobbies, although he did occasionally go fishing when the weather was fine; he certainly didn't have a shotgun or driver's license. His chief enjoyment seemed to be his weekly visit to Fuji or another bar that he frequented.

His schedule had been the same for years and as far as the police could tell, it hadn't changed in the slightest respect since the bank robbery on December eighth.

At headquarters the detectives were looking at the dossier they had prepared on Suzuki. He was five feet five inches tall, of average build, had a long face, and was rather swarthy in complexion.

"Well, going by his build, we can rule him out as being the man with the gun or the man with the drug, and he hasn't got a gold tooth either."

"From what we know of his character I can't really picture him as the leader anyway. I'd say that if he was mixed up in this at all, he would have to be the man with the knife."

"Personally, I can't see him as a member of the gang—he seems too much of a loner to me."

The detectives all tended to think he was innocent. Lieutenant Kaizuka wasn't quite convinced.

"We can't escape the fact that he was in possession of one of the missing banknotes. From our inquiries among the staff at Fuji I think we are all agreed that it was Suzuki who passed the note and on top of that, he hasn't got an alibi for the time of the robbery. December the eighth was a holiday at the temple, and although we can't find any connection between him and the bank, I should think that after walking past it every day for the last twenty years, he should have a good idea of how many people work there and what time the staff would get back."

The detective from the prefectural police thought the same.

"Yes, and also there is no other way that Suzuki could have got hold of the money. As far as we can tell, he has no other income outside his wages from the temple, he doesn't gamble, and no one else in his family is working, so I think there can be only one explanation."

The temple transferred its employees' wages directly into their bank accounts, and although Suzuki had drawn his at the end of the year, the police had checked with the bank and they claimed it was impossible for them to have given him that note. The only logical explanation was that he had been one of the gang and had received the note as part of his share. A month after the robbery, when everything seemed to have quieted down, he probably felt that it was safe to use it.

Sato looked around the assembled detectives and said, "Anyway, I propose that we continue our surveillance for a while longer. He doesn't seem to realize we are watching him, so there's still a chance he will use another of the notes or get in touch with the rest of the gang.

"I think if we pull him in for questioning, we might scare off the leader and he's the one we're after. Even though we haven't seen any sign of the rest of the gang, we don't know in what way he's connected with them and we don't want to show our hand too soon."

Sato's suggestion met with the approval of the other officers and as a result the discovery of the note was kept secret and the surveillance was continued.

But Toho City is a small town and however careful the police were in their inquiries, the rumor soon started that Suzuki was being investigated. Someone at the Fuji told one of the other customers that Suzuki had passed one of the stolen notes in the bar and soon after that Suzuki stopped going there and didn't even visit the other bar he had been a regular at.

He would go straight home from the temple and stay indoors, not even venturing into the garden where he might be seen.

Some of the younger detectives began to feel that it was pointless to hold back and said the suspect should be asked to come to the station to answer their questions or that they should search his house. They argued that now that he knew they were suspicious of him, he wasn't likely to use any more of the stolen money; but if they could find even one more note in his house, they could arrest him on the spot.

However, their superiors couldn't agree with this approach because even if he was one of the gang, they were all agreed that he wasn't the leader, and if they were to search the house, they might scare off the other two. Not only this, but there was no guarantee there were any more stolen notes in Suzuki's house, and they might lose the only lead they had. As long as they waited long enough, as long as they were patient, the criminals were sure to give themselves away.

Almost a fortnight after they started to keep Suzuki under surveillance, he made a move. Although January the nineteenth was a Friday, Suzuki, who had taken the previous Sunday off, went to work as usual. He arrived back home at 4:50 in the afternoon, and the two detectives who had been assigned to him both settled back for an uneventful night until he made his next appearance the following morning.

However at 9:45 that night they were surprised to see Suzuki open the back door and slip out. He was wearing a dark overcoat with the collar turned up, and with both hands thrust into the pockets he hurried off.

The two detectives followed his silhouette and after a short while they realized he was headed for the temple, although he was using the gloomy back streets instead of the main road that he usually took when he went to work.

He seemed to be deep in thought, although he would occasionally pause and look back as if to make sure he wasn't being followed. When he did so, the detectives hid until he moved on again. They both felt the excitement building up inside of them as they were now sure that Suzuki was going to rendezvous with his accomplices.

After a short while he turned into the approach to the temple, and passing under the swooping roof of the main gate, he made his way toward the copper-roofed building that served as the temple office where he worked every day.

There was a light on in the building and judging by the ease with which Suzuki opened the door, it would seem that it hadn't been locked up for the night. The detectives thought this a bit odd and moved to the parking lot where they could keep an eye on the entrance. There were five cars parked there, and among them they recognized the dark red Mercedes which belonged to the Bishop.

The Bishop didn't live on the temple grounds and was driven there every morning by his chauffeur. The other cars belonged to the temple's priests and while the police were watching, another car pulled in bearing the temple's deacon. He was well-known in the town as an astute businessman and the police had no trouble in recognizing his silhouette; but they could not help but notice that he looked more than a little upset as he hurried into the office.

Two more cars pulled into the parking lot and as their occupants walked up to the building, the police recognized them as also being priests of the temple.

No one else turned up and while they couldn't hear any sounds from the illuminated room, the two detectives were certain that a secret conference was going on. It seemed strange to them that Suzuki would be included, but they guessed the meeting had probably been called to resolve some problem that involved him.

About an hour later the meeting ended and they all came out separately. There were at least ten of them altogether, with some having come on foot; but none seemed to be talking, and all walked their separate ways. Finally Suzuki came out and, putting on his overcoat again, he walked away deep in thought. He seemed to be depressed and didn't give a second thought to any possible follower as he made his way down the main street toward his home.

The next day the other detectives connected with the case were all excited by the news.

"I've suspected this ever since we first got a lead on Suzuki," one of the younger men said enthusiastically. "The temple was behind the crime from the beginning! Although it was only some of the people at the bottom of the scale who actually committed the crime,

I can't help but suspect that it was the higher priests who planned the whole thing."

"We also had the report that the getaway car was seen heading in the direction of the temple."

The chief inspector, however, didn't agree. Folding his arms and shaking his head he said, "But Rinko is so wealthy that most other temples would give anything to change places with it. They get more than a hundred million in contributions at New Year and during the summer festival. That's not to mention what they must earn for funerals and memorial services. On top of it all, their income is of a religious nature and completely tax-free.

"There isn't any building going on at the moment, so all the money goes to maintenance and wages. I can't really see any need for them to rob a bank. You only have to look at the way the priests live, with their big houses and a new car every year, to understand that they're not hard up."

Most of the detectives seemed to agree that it was unlikely that the priests at Rinko would endanger their future like that.

"But even if the priests weren't connected, it doesn't necessarily rule out the fact that the crime may have been committed by Suzuki and a couple of his colleagues."

"Their superiors may have found out about it and are trying to think of some way to cover it up. After all, if word got out that it was three employees from the temple who were responsible, it would not do much for the temple's public image."

"Maybe the temple doesn't know that we suspect Suzuki of the bank job, but they heard that we were investigating him and called him in to ask him why."

"You've got a point there."

They could picture Suzuki standing before the priests being questioned about his possible connection with the robbery and as to how and why he had the 10,000-yen note.

It was the answers to these questions that the police wanted, but the only way that they could get them would be to bring him in and interrogate him. But they were beginning to hold the opinion that if Suzuki was a member of the gang, the other two had to be employed at the temple as well, as he didn't appear to have any friends outside the temple. Therefore if they arrested Suzuki, the heads of the temple would destroy the evidence and arrange alibis for the other two in an effort to protect the temple's reputation. If this happened, all Suzuki had to do was say that he had found the note in the street and the whole case would have to be dropped for lack of evidence.

The police decided that for the moment they would just continue with their investigation of Suzuki's background, focusing on possible acquaintances, and once they had enough evidence to build a strong case they would raid the temple and arrest the three men. For the moment, however, they thought it sufficient that they had been able to tie in the temple with Suzuki.

It was two days later that the detectives at Toho City police station were surprised by the news that the bank robbers had been arrested in Oda City. The report came from the prefectural headquarters and stated that at approximately three o'clock in the afternoon of the twenty-second of January a young man in a mah-jongg parlor had asked the cashier to change a 10,000-yen note in order to pay for some noodles he had had delivered.

When she had a chance, the girl at the register checked the serial number, and seeing that it was one on her list, rang the police. Two detectives hurried over and found a young man who looked as if he was in his late teens. When one of the officers asked him a few questions the young man tried to escape but was overpowered and searched. The police found eight more bills whose serial numbers corresponded with those from the robbery. The young man was arrested.

After being questioned, he confessed that he had robbed the bank on the eighth of December and gave them the names and addresses of his two accomplices. These two were arrested and both confessed. The leader was twenty-six years old, unemployed, the other was a twenty-three-year-old factory worker, and the boy who was caught in the mah-jongg parlor was nineteen years old and unemployed.

They told how they had passed through Toho City two or three times on their way to Tokyo and for some reason the bank there had stuck in their minds. After they decided to rob it, they borrowed the shotgun and car from friends, and the leader had gone to the bank once to check it out. Of the twenty million yen that they stole, the leader took eight million and the other two, six million each. They began to use the old notes to pay off their debts and enjoy themselves, and when these ran out, they started to spend the new ones.

First, they tested one of the new notes on January the first, and after waiting until the fifteenth for a reaction, decided the notes were safe to use. They had been passing them ever since without anyone saying anything, so they were surprised when one of them had been caught at the mah-jongg parlor.

The leader seemed to be proud of the way he had tested the money, and on being asked about it, he answered, "I went to Rinko temple on my own on the first and put one of the notes into the offertory box. I knew that the money would be taken to the bank and that if they had a record of the serial numbers there would be some kind of reaction. However, we didn't hear anything after that and decided it must be safe to use the remainder of our money. I suppose the main reason I chose the temple was that there would be nothing to connect me with the money; also, I wanted to offer the money to Buddha so he would save us from getting caught. It doesn't seem to have helped us very much."

The police checked their stories and came to the conclusion they were telling the truth and had been responsible for the crime. They insisted they didn't know Suzuki and although the police made every effort to find a connection, their inquiries proved fruitless. This could only mean that Suzuki had stolen the 10,000-yen note that he had used in the Fuji bar and that it was the one the leader had put in the offertory box at Rinko Temple. In order to check this part of the leader's story, Sato and a constable went to Rinko temple to discuss it with Suzuki.

They asked for Suzuki at the office and heard that he had been called to the main temple by the deacon. The two policemen made their way over there and found the Bishop in the middle of conducting the morning service. He was sitting in front of the central effigy, leading the prayers, and on both sides of him ten younger priests joined in the chant. The two policemen could see the deacon in the hall, but they couldn't see any sign of Suzuki. They decided to wait until the priests finished their devotions.

Sato was standing next to the huge offertory box, and looking at it he thought of the one hundred million yen that had been thrown into it by pilgrims during the New Year holiday, and in particular of the 10,000-yen note that the bank robber had dropped in when he prayed that he wouldn't be caught.

However, the main hall was quite a distance from the office and not only that, but during the New Year holiday it would have been so full of people that Sato felt it most unlikely that Suzuki could have stolen the money.

About thirty minutes later the service came to an end, and as the priests filed out, the deacon noticed the two policemen. He looked at Sato for a moment, then exchanged a glance with the Bishop who also looked at Sato. Seeing this, Sato couldn't help but feel that some kind of message had passed between the Bishop and the deacon.

After the priests had followed the Bishop out of the building, the deacon slowly came over to the policemen. He was a fat man wearing yellow buddhist robes, but his shifty eyes, double chin, and poor complexion made it plain that he was more accustomed to making money than to saving souls.

"I'm from the Toho police station," Sato said, but the deacon seemed to know him and didn't show any surprise.

"What can I do for you?"

"We would like to speak to Mr. Suzuki."

"I think you'll find Suzuki in the office."

"We inquired there first but were directed over here."

"That's strange. I called him over here before the service, but he should have returned quite a while ago."

The deacon gave them a puzzled look.

But Suzuki hadn't returned to the office and although the other workers all joined in the search, he could not be found.

"He may have gone home for something," one of the clerks suggested, but when Sato rang his house, his wife said she hadn't heard from him. Sato had a sudden premonition and hurried over to the house. Suzuki's wife, Miyako, was waiting outside, and seeing the car, ran over and asked, "Have you found him?"

"No. You haven't heard anything either?"

"No, he hasn't been here."

Miyako shook her head, then clutching Sato's arm she said imploringly, "Please find my husband—he might have—"

It was about an hour later when one of the policemen who had joined the search found Suzuki's body hanging from a tree in the woods behind the temple. He had tied a hemp rope to the branch of an oak tree and hanged himself. It was about two hours since he died and this would coincide with the time he left the main hall to return to the office.

His clothes were unruffled and his shoes neatly placed at the foot of the tree, so it seemed most unlikely that he had been attacked. The only strange thing was that he had taken his socks off and put them in his shoes before he hanged himself, and the surrounding area was so covered with his footprints that it almost seemed as if he had made them on purpose.

After the body had been taken to a nearby hospital for an autopsy, Sato took Miyako to the police station and led her into a small room.

"Have you any idea why your husband committed suicide?" Sato asked Miyako in a quiet voice.

She didn't answer and sat chewing her lip, deep in thought.

The police hadn't found a suicide note and although they asked the other people at the temple, they all replied that they had no idea why he should do something like that. But judging from the way in which Miyako had begged him to look for her husband, Sato thought she might have reason to suspect something.

"Didn't you half expect this to happen?"

Miyako still didn't answer and gazed into space in silence, her eyes swollen with crying.

"Even if your husband didn't actually tell you he was going to kill himself, you must have known if he was worried about something. Personally, I get the feeling that your husband was trying to give us a message. I don't think he left those footprints in the mud by accident, but I'm afraid I don't know what he was driving at."

Miyako looked up slowly and after staring at Sato for a few minutes she seemed to make up her mind.

"I think he was trying to make us think of the 'sole of the foot'."

"What?"

"I think he left all those footprints in an effort to lead us to them."

Her eyes gradually came into focus and she seemed, if anything, more grief-stricken than before.

"I see now how much he must have suffered to have chosen this way to try and tell us what he could never have brought himself to say while he was still alive. It's the same as if they had killed him themselves!"

She almost shouted the last words and then collapsed to the table, her whole body wrenched by sobs of sorrow and frustration.

Sato waited until she subsided, then forcing himself to sound calm, he asked, "Who did you mean by that?"

"The Bishop, the deacon, and all the other people in charge of the temple."

"Why would they want to do that to your husband?"

"Because he knew about the 'sole of the foot'."

"Just what exactly do you mean by this 'sole of the foot'?"

Miyako wiped her eyes, then took a deep breath. "Only a few people at the temple use the expression now, but originally it referred to the New Year of festivals when the temple was very crowded. The people would hide the money that didn't go into the offertory box with the soles of their feet and steal it when no one was watching."

"I see, but why do you say only a few people at the temple know its meaning now?"

"These days it refers to the way in which the priests share the offerings among themselves. My husband once told me that it was the same at all the big temples.

"Every year the papers announce how many people visited the temple and how much money was donated, but in reality the temples have decided on these figures in advance and all the money above this estimate is divided among the priests. It's been going on for years now, and they refer to it among themselves as the 'sole of the foot'."

Sato nodded to himself as he realized the full significance of the footprints, then his mind went back to the deacon's fat face and the chauffeur-driven cars.

"The papers estimated that 1,700,000 people visited the temple this New Year, and donated approximately 100,000,000 yen. But my husband told me that while the temple actually received 120,000,000 yen, it announced a total of only 80,000,000."

"Do you mean that the priests divided the remaining forty million between them?"

"Yes. Their shares were set a long time ago. If I remember rightly, the chief priest gets fifteen percent, the deacon and three other high priests get ten percent each, and the remainder is divided among the other priests. My husband and other section chiefs are given a small bonus."

"That would mean that the chief priest got six million . . . and you say that he embezzles that much every New Year and festival? How much did your husband get? About one million?"

"He told me that he was given 750,000 yen this year, but in his case it was rather to keep him from talking than anything else. The whole system was a well guarded secret at the temple and they weren't allowed to talk about it even to their families. We'd been married for ten years before my husband finally told me about it."

"How did he get the money? In cash?"

"Yes. On the third of January the financial department starts to count the donations in a basement room of the temple. The chief priest, the deacon, and the other high priests are all present while this is being done, and as soon as they have reached the official amount, they divide the extra between them. My husband and the priests who weren't present at the counting wait in a separate room, and when the count is finished, their shares are brought out to them."

"I suppose the 10,000-yen note in question was part of your husband's share?"

"Yes, I can't think of any other explanation."

The stolen 10,000-yen note had found its way from the offertory box to Suzuki's pocket, but he, not knowing that it was stolen, had used it quite openly at the Fuji bar. When the temple leaders learned that Suzuki was being watched by the police, they must have become very worried. The meeting the police had witnessed was obviously called in order to decide what the temple should do to cover itself and not be connected with the bank robbery.

"What was your husband told to tell the police if he was asked where he got the 10,000-yen note?"

"First, the deacon told him to say he found it in the street, but when it was announced in the papers that one of the thieves had donated the money to the temple—"

"Yes, what was he to say then? No one would believe he had found it in the street."

"For two days now, ever since the report appeared in the papers, he has been called by the chief priest and deacon countless times and ordered to say that he stole the money from the offertory box. In that way only he would be faced with a scandal and the temple would remain safe.

"Of course he couldn't continue to work at the temple after that, but they promised him that although they would have to discharge him, they would guarantee his wages for the rest of his life.

"As I understand it, by not declaring all their income they are guilty of embezzlement and not only they but the temple itself would not be likely to survive the scandal if the facts became public. They tried to frighten my husband, saying that not only would Rinko temple be ruined but all the big temples would come under scrutiny and it would be the end of religion in Japan. They told him that it would be best for everyone if he was to say he stole the money, but that Buddha knew the truth and would protect him.

"That's why he was called to the main temple before the service this morning—to persuade him to take the blame.

"I'm sure that was it. My husband was always very timid, but he was also an honest man. He didn't like to take the money in the first place, but he realized that if he was going to work in the temple, he would have to go along with its customs. However, when he was told to pretend he'd stolen the money, it was too much for him.

Even though they told him they would look after him for life, it would leave a stain on his character that he could never get rid of."

Miyako shuddered as she thought of the anguish her husband had had to bear.

"But I don't think he had the strength to expose the plot either, so in the end he settled the problem by sacrificing himself for the greed of the priests. But leaving all those footprints around the tree as a clue, I think that deep down he really wanted to bring the case out into the open."

Sato could still visualize the footprints under the body hanging from the oak tree. Suzuki had made them carefully, using his whole weight to imprint his bitterness in the mud.

Lieutenant Sato saw that he too would have to proceed carefully, step by step, if he wanted to find the proof necessary to convict the leaders of such a large and famous temple of so serious and shocking a crime.

Sato suddenly stood up and, walking over to the window, gave a deep sigh. All he could see outside were a few lonely snowflakes falling to the empty stone-paved approach to the temple.